Mark Kritzman

The Portable Financial Analyst

What Practitioners Need to Know

from
The Financial Analysts Journal
The Association for Investment Management and Research

IRWIN
Professional Publishing®
Chicago • London • Singapore

This publication is designed to provide accurate and authoritative information in regard to the subject matter covered. It is sold with the understanding that the author and the publisher are not engaged in rendering legal, accounting, or other professional service.

ISBN 1-55738-831-8

Printed in the United States of America

BB

3 4 5 6 7 8 9 0

TAQ/BJS

Table of Contents

Foreword

by Peter L. Bernstein

Karl Marx summed up the whole process of capitalism in three simple letters: M–C–M′. Capitalists begin with money, invest in capital, and end up with more money than they started with. At least, that is their goal.

The voyage from M to M′ can be long, short, straight, circuitous, upward, downward, bumpy, or smooth. Marx filled three volumes of writing to explain that the investor's arrival at M′ is never certain because of forces over which the capitalist has no control.

Capitalists who choose to place their M in assets acquired in the financial markets will own a C whose ultimate conversion into M′ is even more chancy than capitalists who invest in real assets. Most financial assets are acquired by buying from another investor. Most financial assets are converted back into M′ by selling to another investor.

One never knows how accommodating those other investors are going to be when the moment to act arrives, because the investor on the other side of a transaction also faces unknown forces. Debt securities are less risky than equities in this sense, because they promise a payoff outside the financial markets, but the ability of the borrower to redeem, and the purchasing power of the M′ at the appointed moment, are also uncertain; in any case, investors acquire and liquidate debt securities in the markets far more then in direct transactions with borrowers. Investing in real assets is also risky, but business managers have far more control over the costs of production and the motivation of their customers.

In this book, Mark Kritzman has provided us with an operating manual to guide us on this perilous passage through the financial markets from M to M′. His essays go to the very core of the investor's dilemma: how to make decisions in the face of unknown forces without succumbing to helplessness, and how to assert some control over the outcome without succumbing to hubris. Kritzman teaches us that helplessness is unnecessary and that hubris is folly.

Many other books promise to accomplish the same thing, but they fall short on one of two scores. Some lack rigor, which means that they are unreliable or inconsistent. Others focus on rigor to a degree that makes them incomprehensible to people faced with the daily task of making decisions in the real world. Kritzman avoids both extremes by combining a rare degree of lucidity with impeccable logic. Clarity emerges from material that seldom bends to simplicity.

The book demonstrates how investors can—indeed, must—employ the tools of mathematics, statistics, and ultimately just plain common sense to negotiate a safe arrival on the journey from M to C and from C to M'. Kritzman reveals why uncertainty is not the same thing as mystery. In the area where numbers are dominant, he instructs us how to measure what we are doing, what others are doing, and what all of us might be doing under different environments. He articulates the inescapable trade-off between risk and return, which begins with measurement and ends with optimizing their conflicting consequences. He never allows us to lose sight of the power of time in the whole process: every chapter reminds us that time as well as capital separates M from M'.

I share Kritzman's conviction that a practitioner is soon lost without the support of theory: the material in this book is what practitioners need to know. The key work is "need." Woe to the practitioner who does not know what is here.

Preface

In the fall of 1990 I was invited by Chuck D'Ambrosio to write the column, "What Practitioners Need to Know" for the *Financial Analysts Journal*. During the next several years, I wrote 21 articles covering a variety of technical topics that I thought would be of interest to the readers of the *FAJ*. This book is a collection of those articles.

Over the years, I have tried to select topics that I thought were confusing and sometimes controversial, with the hope of instilling clarity and promoting consensus. My presumed audience was the typical financial analyst who I often describe as a "dilequant"; that is, one who dabbles in quantitative methods. I have thus made an effort to avoid unnecessary technical jargon and to substitute numerical examples for mathematical symbolism. Moreover, I have attempted to write self-contained articles so that the reader would be spared the task of consulting additional references.

There is no particular design to the order in which the articles appeared in the *FAJ*. I began by writing about topics that were familiar to me, which I discovered to be a quickly exhaustible list. Additional topics were suggested to me by *FAJ* readers and friends in the investment community, and some topics were inspired by my own research and participation at seminars.

In this book, I have organized the chapters into three broad groups: Concepts, Methodology, and Strategy, although some of the chapters could easily have been assigned to more than one group. The chapters assigned to the Concepts section deal with theories and ideas that form the foundation of financial analysis. The Methodology section includes chapters that have more of a "how to" flavor. The section on Strategy addresses particular portfolio management applications. Please do not attach too much importance to this organization. You should feel comfortable reading the chapters in any sequence.

In preparing these columns, I have been the beneficiary of helpful advice from many sources. I particularly wish to acknowledge the comments of Carl Benning, Peter Bernstein, Stephen Brown, George Chow, Robert Ferguson, John Harris, Ira Kawaller, Bruce Lehman, William Margrabe, Jack Meyer, Dan Nelson, Krishna Ramaswamy, Gita Rao, William Sharpe, and Richard Tanenbaum. Obviously, they are not accountable for any errors.

I wish to express my gratitude to Brian Singer and Kevin Terhaar who read the entire manuscript. Their efforts have spared me the embarrassment of many typos and several "thinkos."

During the past five years I received enormous editorial help from Judith Kimball, Managing Editor of the *FAJ*. She has vastly improved every manuscript that I submitted to her.

I wish to express my deep appreciation to Chuck D'Ambrosio for inviting me to write the columns and for his continuing support over the years and to Van Harlow for his continuing support as Editor of the *FAJ*. I also wish to thank the Association for Investment Management and Research for their participation in this project.

My final thanks are for my wife, Elizabeth Gorman, who has happily endured my bi-monthly anxiety about selecting a topic as each submission date approached.

Mark Kritzman
Cambridge

PART I

CONCEPTS

The Nobel Prize

On October 16, 1990, the Royal Swedish Academy of Sciences announced its selection for the Nobel Memorial Prize in Economic Science. For the first time since the prize for economics was established in 1968, the Royal Academy chose three individuals whose primary contributions are in finance and whose affiliations are not with arts and science schools, but rather with schools of business. Harry Markowitz was cited for his pioneering research in portfolio selection, while William Sharpe shared the award for developing an equilibrium theory of asset pricing. Merton Miller was a co-winner for his contributions in corporate finance, in which he showed, along with Franco Modigliani, that the value of a firm should be invariant to its capital structure and dividend policy.

The pioneering research of these individuals revolutionized finance and motivated the application of quantitative methods to financial analysis.

Portfolio Selection

In his classic article, "Portfolio Selection," Markowitz submitted that investors should not choose portfolios that maximize expected return, because this criterion by itself ignores the principle of diversification.[1] He proposed that investors should instead consider variances of return, along with expected returns, and choose portfolios that offer the highest expected return for a given level of variance. He called this rule the E-V maxim.

Markowitz showed that a portfolio's expected return is simply the weighted average of the expected returns of its component securities. A portfolio's variance is a more complicated concept, however. It depends on more than just the variances of the component securities.

The variance of an individual security is a measure of the dispersion of its returns. It is calculated by squaring the difference between each return in a series and the mean return for the series, then averaging these squared differences. (The square root of the variance, or the standard deviation, is often used in practice because it measures dispersion in the same units the underlying return is measured in.)

Variance provides a reasonable gauge of a security's risk, but the average of the variances of two securities will not necessarily give a good indication of the risk of a portfolio comprising these two securities. The portfolio's risk depends also on the extent to which the two securities move together—that is, the extent to which their prices react in like fashion to a particular event.

To quantify comovement among security returns, Markowitz introduced the statistical concept of covariance. The covariance between two securities equals the standard deviation of the first times the standard deviation of the second times the correlation coefficient between the two.

The correlation coefficient, in this context, measures the association between the returns of two securities. It ranges in value from 1 to –1. If one security's returns are higher than its average return when another security's returns are higher than its average return, for example, the correlation coefficient will be positive, somewhere between 0 and 1. Alternatively, if one security's returns are lower than its average return when another security's returns are higher than its average return, then the correlation coefficient will be negative.

The correlation coefficient, by itself, is an inadequate measure of covariance because it measures only the direction and degree of association between securities' returns. It does not account for the magnitude of variability in each security's returns. Covariance captures magnitude by multiplying the correlation coefficient by the standard deviations of the securities' returns.

Consider, for example, the covariance of a security with itself. Obviously, the correlation coefficient in this case equals 1. A security's covariance with itself thus equals the standard deviation of its returns squared (which, of course, is its variance).

Finally, portfolio variance depends also on the weightings of its constituent securities—the proportion of portfolio market value invested in each. The variance of a portfolio consisting of two securities equals the variance of the first security times its weighting squared plus the variance of the second security times its weighting squared plus twice the covariance between the securities times each security's weighting. The standard deviation of this portfolio equals the square root of the variance.

From this formulation of portfolio risk, Markowitz was able to offer two key insights. First, unless the securities in a portfolio are perfectly inversely correlated (i.e., have a correlation coefficient of −1), it is not possible to eliminate portfolio risk entirely through diversification. If we divide a portfolio equally among its component securities, for example, as the number of securities in the portfolio increases, the portfolio's risk will tend not toward zero but, rather, toward the average covariance of the component securities.

Second, unless all the securities in a portfolio are perfectly positively correlated with each other (a correlation coefficient of 1), a portfolio's standard deviation will always be less than the weighted average standard deviation of its component securities. Consider, for example, a portfolio consisting of two securities, both of which have expected returns of 10 percent and standard deviations of 20 percent and which are uncorrelated with each other. If we allocate portfolio assets equally between these two securities, the portfolio's expected return will equal 10 percent, while its standard deviation will equal 14.14 percent. The portfolio offers a reduction in risk of nearly 30 percent relative to investment in either of the two securities separately. Moreover, this risk reduction is achieved without any sacrifice of expected return.

Markowitz also demonstrated that, for given levels of risk, we can identify particular combinations of securities that maximize expected return. He deemed these portfolios "efficient" and referred to a continuum of such portfolios in dimensions of expected return and standard deviation as the *efficient frontier*. According to Markowitz's E-V maxim, investors should restrict their choice of portfolio to those that are located along the efficient frontier. It is almost always the case that there exists some portfolio on the efficient frontier that offers a higher expected return and less risk than the least risky of its component securities (assuming the least risky security is not completely riskless).

The financial community was slow to implement Markowitz's theory, in large part because of practical constraints. In order to estimate the risk of a portfolio of securities, one must estimate the variances of every security, along with the covariances between every pair of securities. For a portfolio of 100 securities, this means calculating 100 variances and 4,950 covariances—5,050 risk estimates! In general, the number of required risk estimates (variances and covariances) equals n(n + 1) / 2, where n equals the number of securities in the portfolio.[2] In 1952, when Markowitz published "Portfolio Selection," the sheer number of calculations formed an obstacle in the way of acceptance. It was in part the challenge of this obstacle that motivated William Sharpe to develop a single index measure of a security's risk.

The Capital Asset Pricing Model

James Tobin, the 1981 winner of the Nobel Prize in economics, showed that the investment process can be separated into two distinct steps—(1) the construction of an efficient portfolio, as described by Markowitz, and (2) the decision to combine this efficient portfolio with a riskless investment. This two-step process is the famed separation theorem.[3]

Sharpe extended Markowitz's and Tobin's insights to develop a theory of market equilibrium under conditions of risk.[4] First, Sharpe showed that there is along the efficient frontier a unique portfolio that, when combined with lending or borrowing at the pure interest rate (Treasury-bill rate), dominates all other combinations of efficient portfolios and lending or borrowing.

Figure 1.1 shows a two-dimensional graph, with risk represented by the horizontal axis and expected return represented by the vertical axis. The efficient frontier appears as the positively sloped concave curve. The straight line emanating from the vertical axis at the pure interest rate illustrates the efficient frontier with borrowing and lending. The segment of the line between the vertical axis and the efficient portfolio curve represents some combination of the efficient portfolio and lending at the pure interest rate, while points along the straight line to the right represent some combination of the efficient portfolio and borrowing at the pure interest rate. Combinations of portfolio O and lending or borrowing at the pure interest rate will always offer the highest expected rate of return for a given level of risk.

With two assumptions, Sharpe demonstrated that in equilibrium investors will prefer points along the line emanating from the pure interest rate that is tangent to O. The requisite assumptions are that (1) there exists a single pure interest rate at which investors can lend and borrow in unlimited amounts and (2) investors have homogene-

Figure 1.1   Efficient Frontier with Borrowing and Lending

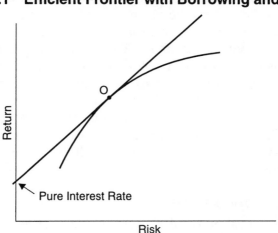

ous expectations regarding expected returns, variances and correlations. Under these assumptions, Sharpe showed that portfolio O is the market portfolio, which represents the maximum achievable diversification.

Within this paradigm, Sharpe proceeded to demonstrate that risk can be partitioned into two sources—that caused by changes in the value of the market portfolio, which cannot be diversified away, and that caused by non-market factors, which is diversified away in the market portfolio. He labeled the non-diversifiable risk *systematic risk* and the diversifiable risk *unsystematic risk.*

Sharpe also showed that a security's systematic risk can be estimated by regressing its returns (less the pure interest rate) against the market portfolio's returns (less the pure interest rate). The slope from this regression equation, which Sharpe called beta, quantifies the security's systematic risk when multiplied by the market risk. The unexplained variation in the security's return (the residuals from the regression equation) represents the security's unsystematic risk. He then asserted that, in an efficient market, investors are only compensated for bearing systematic risk, because it cannot be diversified away, and that the expected return of a security is, through beta, linearly related to the market's expected return.

It is important to distinguish between a single index model and the Capital Asset Pricing Model (CAPM). A single index model does not require that the intercept of the regression equation (alpha) equal 0 percent. It simply posits a single source of systematic, or common, risk. (Stated differently, the residuals from the regression equation are uncorrelated with each other.) The important practical implication is that it is not necessary to estimate covariances between securities. Each security's contribution to portfolio risk is captured through its beta coefficient. The CAPM, by contrast, does require that the intercept of the regression equation equal 0 percent in an efficient market. The CAPM itself does not necessarily assume a single source of systematic risk. This is tantamount to allowing for some correlation among the residuals.

Invariance Propositions

Between the publication of Markowitz's theory of portfolio selection and Sharpe's equilibrium theory of asset pricing, Franco Modigliani (the 1985 Nobel Prize winner in economics) and Merton Miller published two related articles in which they expounded their now famous invariance propositions. The first, "The Cost of Capital, Corporation Finance, and the Theory of Investment," appeared in 1958.[5] It challenged the then conventional wisdom that a firm's value depends on its capital structure (that is, its debt/equity mix).

In challenging this traditional view, Modigliani and Miller invoked the notion of arbitrage. They argued that if a leveraged firm is undervalued, investors can purchase its debt and its shares. The interest paid by the firm is offset by the interest received by the investors, so the investors end up holding a pure equity stream. Alternatively, if an unleveraged firm is undervalued, investors can borrow funds to purchase its shares. The substitutability of individual debt for corporate debt guarantees that firms in the same risk class will be valued the same, regardless of their respective capital structures. In essence, Modigliani and Miller argued in favor of the law of one price.

In a subsequent article, "Dividend Policy, Growth, and the Valuation of Shares," Modigliani and Miller proposed that a firm's value is invariant, not only to its capital structure, but also to its dividend policy (assuming the firm's investment decision is set independently).[6] Again, they invoked the notion of substitutability, arguing that repurchasing shares has the same effect as paying dividends; thus issuing shares and paying dividends is a wash. Although the cash component of an investor's return may differ as a function of dividend policy, the investor's total return, including price change, should not change with dividend policy.

Modigliani and Miller's invariance propositions have inspired an enormous amount of debate and research. Much of the sometimes spirited debate has centered on the assumption of perfect capital markets. In the real world, where investors cannot borrow and lend at the riskless rate of interest, where both corporations and individuals pay taxes, and where investors do not share equal access with management to relevant information, there is only spotty evidence to support Modigliani and Miller's invariance propositions.

But the value of the contributions of these Nobel laureates does not depend on the degree to which their theories hold in an imperfect market environment. It depends, rather, on the degree to which they changed the financial community's understanding of the capital markets. Markowitz taught us how to evaluate investment opportunities probabilistically, while Sharpe provided us with an equilibrium theory of asset pricing, enabling us to distinguish between risk that is rewarded and risk that is not rewarded. Miller, in collaboration with Modigliani, demonstrated how the simple notion of arbitrage can be applied to determine value; as we all know, this has had a profound impact on subsequent financial analysis. As financial analysts, we owe a great debt to these Nobel laureates.

Notes

1. H. Markowitz, "Portfolio Selection," *Journal of Finance*, March 1952.

2. This same formula gives the sum of $1 + 2 + 3 + \ldots + n$. There is an amusing story about this formula and the famous mathematician Gauss. According to legend, when Gauss was a child just starting school, the teacher asked the students in Gauss' class to add the numbers from one to 100. The teacher's intent was to keep the students busy for a while. But Gauss, after a few seconds, raised his hand with the answer—5,050. The teacher asked him how he had added so quickly. Gauss described how he had begun by adding one plus two plus three but became bored and started adding backward from 100. He then noticed that one plus 100 equals 101, as did

two plus 99 and three plus 98, and realized that if he multiplied 100 by 101 and divided by two (so as not to double-count), he would arrive at the answer.

3. J. Tobin, "Liquidity Preferences as Behavior Toward Risk," *Review of Economic Studies*, February 1958.

4. W. Sharpe, "Capital Asset Prices: A Theory of Market Equilibrium Under Conditions of Uncertainty," *Journal of Finance*, September 1964.

5. F. Modigliani and M. Miller, "The Cost of Capital, Corporation Finance, and the Theory of Investment," *American Economic Review*, June 1958.

6. M. Miller and F. Modigliani, "Dividend Policy, Growth, and the Valuation of Shares," *Journal of Business*, October 1961.

2
Uncertainty

The primary challenge to the financial analyst is to determine how to proceed in the face of uncertainty. Uncertainty arises from imperfect knowledge and from incomplete data. Methods for interpreting limited information may thus help analysts measure and control uncertainty.

Long ago, natural scientists noticed the widespread presence of random variation in nature. This led to the development of laws of probability, which help predict outcomes. As it turns out, many of the laws that seem to explain the behavior of random variables in nature apply as well to the behavior of financial variables such as corporate earnings, interest rates, and asset prices and returns.

Relative Frequency

A random variable can be thought of as an event whose outcome in a given situation depends on chance factors. For example, the toss of a coin is an event whose outcome is governed by chance, as is next year's closing price for the S&P 500. Because an outcome is influenced by chance does not mean that we are completely ignorant about its possible values. We may, for example, be able to garner some insights from prior experiences.

Suppose we are interested in predicting the return of the S&P 500 over the next 12 months. Should we be more confident in predicting that it will be between 0 and 10 percent than between 10 and 20 percent? The past history of returns on the index can tell us how often returns within specified ranges have occurred. Table 2.1 shows the annual returns over the last 40 years.

We can simply count the number of returns between 0 and 10 percent and the number of returns between 10 and 20 percent. Dividing each figure by 40 gives us the *relative frequency* of returns within each range. Six returns fall within the range of 0 to 10 percent, while 10 returns fall within the range of 10 to 20 percent. The relative fre-

Table 2.1 S&P 500 Annual Returns

1951	24.0%	1961	26.9%	1971	14.3%	1981	−4.9%
1952	18.4%	1962	−8.7%	1972	19.0%	1982	21.4%
1953	−1.0%	1963	22.8%	1973	−14.7%	1983	22.5%
1954	52.6%	1964	16.5%	1974	−26.5%	1984	6.3%
1955	31.6%	1965	12.5%	1975	37.2%	1985	32.2%
1956	6.6%	1966	−10.1%	1976	23.8%	1986	18.8%
1957	−10.8%	1967	24.0%	1977	−7.2%	1987	5.3%
1958	43.4%	1968	11.1%	1978	6.6%	1988	16.6%
1959	12.0%	1969	−8.5%	1979	18.4%	1989	31.8%
1960	0.5%	1970	4.0%	1980	32.4%	1990	−3.1%

Source: Data through 1981 from R. Ibbotson and R. Sinquefield, *Stocks, Bonds, Bills and Inflation: The Past and the Future* (Charlottesville, VA: The Financial Analysts Research Foundation, 1982).

quencies of these observations are 15 and 25 percent, respectively, as Table 2.2 shows.

Figure 2.1 depicts this information graphically in what is called a *discrete probability distribution.* (It is discrete because it covers a finite number of observations.) The values along the vertical axis represent the probability (equal here to the relative frequency) of observing a return within the ranges indicated along the horizontal axis.

The information we have is limited. For one thing, the return ranges (which we set) are fairly wide. For another, the sample is

Table 2.2 Frequency Distribution

Range of Return	Frequency	Relative Frequency
-30% to -20%	1	2.5%
-20% to -10%	3	7.5%
-10% to 0%	6	15.0%
0% to 10%	6	15.0%
10% to 20%	10	25.0%
20% to 30%	7	17.5%
30% to 40%	5	12.5%
40% to 50%	1	2.5%
50% to 60%	1	2.5%

Figure 2.1 Discrete Probability Distribution

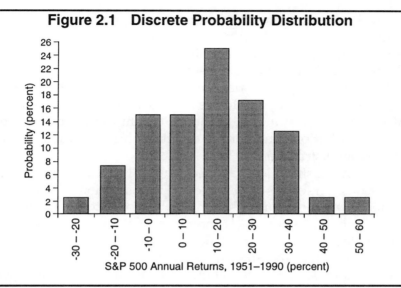

S&P 500 Annual Returns, 1951–1990 (percent)

confined to annual returns and covers only the past 40 years, a period which excludes two world wars and the Great Depression.

We can nonetheless draw several inferences from this limited information. For example, we may assume that we are about two-thirds more likely to observe a return within the range of 10 to 20 percent than a return within the range of 0 to 10 percent. Furthermore, by summing the relative frequencies for the three ranges below 0 percent, we can also assume that there is a 25 percent chance of experiencing a negative return.

If we want to make more precise inferences, we should increase the sample and partition the data into narrower ranges. If we proceed along these lines, the distribution of returns should eventually conform to the familiar pattern known as the bell-shaped curve, or *normal distribution*.

Normal Distribution

The normal distribution is a *continuous probability distribution;* it assumes there are an infinite number of observations covering all possible values along a continuous scale. Time, for example, can be thought of as being distributed along a continuous scale. Stocks, however, trade in units that are multiples of one-eighth, so technically stock returns cannot be distributed continuously. Nonetheless, for purposes of financial analysis, the normal distribution is usually a reasonable approximation of the distribution of stock returns, as well as the returns of other financial assets.

The formula that gives rise to the normal distribution was first published by Abraham de Moivre in 1733. Its properties were investigated by Carl Gauss in the 18th and 19th centuries. In recognition of Gauss' contributions, the normal distribution is often referred to as the Gaussian distribution.

The normal distribution has special appeal to natural scientists for two reasons. First, it is an excellent approximation of the random variation of many natural phenomena.[1] Second, it can be described fully by only two values—(1) the mean of the observations, which measures location or central tendency, and (2) the variance of the observations, which measures dispersion.

For our sample of S&P 500 annual returns, the *mean return* (which is also the expected return) equals the sum of the observed returns times their probabilities of occurrence:

$$\overline{R} = R_1 \cdot P_1 + R_2 \cdot P_2 + ... + R_n \cdot P_n$$

$\overline{R}$ equals the mean return. $R_1, R_2,...R_n$ equal the observed returns in years one through n. $P_1, P_2, ... P_n$ equal the probabilities of occurrence (or relative frequencies) of the returns in years one through n. This computation yields the arithmetic mean. (The arithmetic mean ignores the effects of compounding; I will discuss later how to modify this calculation to account for compounding.)

The *variance* of returns is computed as the average squared difference from the mean. To compute the variance, we subtract the mean return from each annual return, square this value, sum these squared values, and then divide by the number of observations (or n, which in our example equals 40).[2] The formula for variance, V, is:

$$V = \frac{(R_1 - \overline{R})^2 + (R_2 - \overline{R})^2 + ... + (R_n - \overline{R})^2}{n}$$

The square root of the variance, which is called the *standard deviation*, is commonly used as a measure of dispersion.

If we apply these formulas to the annual returns in Table 2.1, we find that the mean return for the sample equals 12.9 percent, the variance of returns equals 2.9 percent, and the standard deviation of returns equals 16.9 percent. These values, together with the assumption that the returns of the S&P 500 are normally distributed, enable us to infer a normal probability distribution of S&P 500 returns. This is shown in Figure 2.2.

The normal distribution has several important characteristics. First, it is symmetric around its mean; 50 percent of the returns are below the mean return and 50 percent of the returns are above the mean return. Also, because of this symmetry, the mode of the sample—the most common observation—and the median—the middle value of the observations—are equal to each other and to the mean.

Note that the area enclosed within one standard deviation on either side of the mean encompasses 68 percent of the total area under the curve. The area enclosed within two standard deviations on either side of the mean encompasses 95 percent of the total area under the curve, and 99.7 percent of the area under the curve falls within plus and minus three standard deviations of the mean.

From this information we are able to draw several conclusions. For example, we know that 68, 95 and 99.7 percent of returns, respectively, will fall within one, two and three standard deviations (plus and minus) of the mean return. It is thus straightforward to measure the probability of experiencing returns that are one, two or three standard deviations away from the mean.

Figure 2.2   Normal Probability Distribution

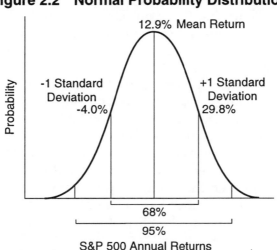

There is, for example, about a 32 percent (100 percent minus 68 percent) chance of experiencing returns at least one standard deviation above or below the mean return. Thus there is only a 16 percent chance of experiencing a return below –4.0 percent (mean of 12.9 percent minus standard deviation of 16.9 percent) and about an equal chance of experiencing a return greater than 29.8 percent (mean of 12.9 percent plus standard deviation of 16.9 percent).

Standardized Variables

We may, however, be interested in the likelihood of experiencing a return of less than 0 percent or a return of greater than 15 percent. In order to determine the probabilities of these returns (or the probability of achieving any return, for that matter), we can standardize the target return. We do so by subtracting the mean return from the target return and dividing by the standard deviation. (By standardizing returns we, in effect, rescale the distribution to have a mean of 0 and a standard deviation of 1.) Thus, to find the area under the curve to the left of 0 percent (which is tantamount to the probability of experiencing a return of less than 0 percent), we subtract 12.9 percent (the mean) from 0 percent (the target) and divide this quantity by 16.9 percent (the standard deviation):

$$\frac{0\% - 12.9\%}{16.9\%} = -0.7633$$

This value tells us that 0 percent is 0.7633 standard deviation below the mean. This is much less than a full standard deviation, so we know that the chance of experiencing a return of less than 0 percent must be greater than 16 percent.

In order to calculate a precise probability directly, we need to evaluate the integral of the standardized normal density function. Fortunately, most statistics books include tables that show the area under a standardized normal distribution curve that corresponds to a particular standardized variable. Table 2.3 is one example.

To find the area under the curve to the left of the standardized variable we read down the left column to the value –0.7 and across this row to the column under the value –0.06. The value at this location—0.2236—equals the probability of experiencing a return of less than 0 percent. This, of course, implies that the chance of experiencing a return greater than 0 percent equals 0.7764 (1 – 0.2236). (The probability of experiencing a negative return as estimated from the discrete probability distribution in Table 2.2 equals 25 percent.)

Suppose we are interested in the likelihood of experiencing an annualized return of less than 0 percent on average over a five-year horizon? First, we'll assume that the year-by-year returns are mutually independent (that is, this year's return has no effect on next year's return). We can then convert the standard deviation back to the variance (by squaring it), divide the variance by five (the years in the horizon) and use the square root of this value to standardize the difference between 0 percent and the mean return. Alternatively, we can simply divide the standard deviation by the square root of five and use this value to standardize the difference:

$$\frac{0\% - 12.9\%}{16.9\%/\sqrt{5}} = -1.71$$

Again, by referring to Table 2.3, we find that the likelihood of experiencing an annualized return of less than 0 percent on average over five years equals only 0.0436, or 4.36 percent. This is much less than the probability of experiencing a negative return in any one year. Intuitively, we are less likely to lose money on average over five years than in any particular year because we are diversifying across time; a loss in any particular year might be offset by a gain in one or more of the other years.

Now suppose we are interested in the likelihood that we might lose money in *one or more* of the five years. This probability is equivalent to one minus the probability of experiencing a positive return in every one of the five years. Again, if we assume independence in the year-to-year returns, the likelihood of experiencing five consecutive yearly returns each greater than 0 percent equals 0.7764 raised to the fifth power, which is 0.2821. Thus the probability of experiencing a negative return in at least one of the five years equals 0.7179 (= 1 − 0.2821).

Over extended holding periods, the normal distribution may not be a good approximation of the distribution of returns because short-holding-period returns are compounded, rather than cumulated, to derive long-holding-period returns. Because we can represent the compound value of an index as a simple accumulation when expressed in terms of logarithms, it is the logarithms of one plus the holding-period returns that are normally distributed. The actual re-

Table 2.3 Normal Distribution Table
(probability that standardized variable is less than z)

z	.00	.01	.02	.03	.04	.05	.06	.07	.08	.09
-3.0	.0013	.0013	.0013	.0012	.0012	.0011	.0011	.0011	.0010	.0010
-2.9	.0019	.0018	.0018	.0017	.0017	.0016	.0015	.0015	.0014	.0014
-2.8	.0026	.0025	.0024	.0023	.0023	.0022	.0021	.0021	.0020	.0019
-2.7	.0035	.0034	.0033	.0032	.0031	.0030	.0029	.0028	.0027	.0026
-2.6	.0047	.0045	.0044	.0043	.0041	.0040	.0039	.0038	.0037	.0036
-2.5	.0062	.0060	.0059	.0057	.0055	.0054	.0052	.0051	.0049	.0048
-2.4	.0082	.0080	.0078	.0075	.0073	.0071	.0069	.0068	.0066	.0064
-2.3	.0107	.0104	.0102	.0099	.0096	.0094	.0091	.0089	.0087	.0084
-2.2	.0139	.0136	.0132	.0129	.0125	.0122	.0119	.0116	.0113	.0110
-2.1	.0179	.0174	.0170	.0166	.0162	.0158	.0154	.0150	.0146	.0143
-2.0	.0228	.0222	.0217	.0212	.0207	.0202	.0197	.0192	.0188	.0183
-1.9	.0287	.0281	.0275	.0268	.0262	.0256	.0250	.0244	.0239	.0233
-1.8	.0359	.0351	.0344	.0336	.0329	.0322	.0314	.0307	.0300	.0294
-1.7	.0446	.0436	.0427	.0418	.0409	.0401	.0392	.0384	.0375	.0367
-1.6	.0548	.0537	.0526	.0516	.0505	.0495	.0485	.0475	.0465	.0455
-1.5	.0668	.0655	.0643	.0630	.0618	.0606	.0594	.0582	.0571	.0560
-1.4	.0808	.0793	.0778	.0764	.0750	.0735	.0721	.0708	.0694	.0681
-1.3	.0968	.0951	.0934	.0918	.0901	.0885	.0869	.0853	.0838	.0823
-1.2	.1151	.1131	.1112	.1093	.1075	.1056	.1038	.1020	.1003	.0985
-1.1	.1357	.1335	.1314	.1292	.1271	.1251	.1230	.1210	.1190	.1170
-1.0	.1587	.1562	.1539	.1515	.1492	.1469	.1446	.1423	.1401	.1379
-0.9	.1841	.1814	.1788	.1762	.1736	.1711	.1685	.1660	.1635	.1611
-0.8	.2119	.2090	.2061	.2033	.2005	.1977	.1949	.1921	.1894	.1867
-0.7	.2420	.2389	.2358	.2327	.2296	.2266	.2236	.2206	.2177	.2148
-0.6	.2743	.2709	.2676	.2643	.2611	.2578	.2546	.2514	.2483	.2451
-0.5	.3085	.3050	.3015	.2981	.2946	.2912	.2877	.2843	.2810	.2776
-0.4	.3446	.3400	.3372	.3336	.3300	.3264	.3228	.3192	.3156	.3121
-0.3	.3821	.3783	.3745	.3707	.3669	.3632	.3694	.3557	.3520	.3483
-0.2	.4207	.4168	.4129	.4090	.4052	.4013	.3974	.3936	.3897	.3859
-0.1	.4602	.4562	.4522	.4483	.4443	.4404	.4364	.4325	.4286	.4247
-0.0	.5000	.4960	.4920	.4880	.4840	.4801	.4761	.4721	.4681	.4641

turns thus conform to a lognormal distribution. A lognormal distribution assigns higher probabilities to extremely high values than it does to extremely low values; the result is a skewed distribution, rather than a symmetric one. This distinction is usually not significant for holding periods of one year or less. For longer holding periods, the distinction can be important. For this reason, we should assume a lognormal distribution when estimating the probabilities associated with outcomes over long investment horizons.[3]

Caveats

In applying the normal probability distribution to measure uncertainty in financial analysis, we should proceed with caution. We must recognize, for example, that our probability estimates are subject to sampling error. Our example assumed implicitly that the experience from 1951 through 1990 characterized the mean and variance of returns for the S&P 500. This period, in fact, represents but a small sample of the entire universe of historical returns and may not necessarily be indicative of the central tendency and dispersion of returns going forward.

As an alternative to extrapolating historical data, we can choose to estimate S&P 500 expected returns based on judgmental factors. We can infer the investment community's consensus prediction of the standard deviation from the prices of options on the S&P 500.[4]

Finally, we must remember that the normal distribution and the lognormal distribution are not perfect models of the distribution of asset returns and other financial variables. They are, in many circumstances, reasonable approximations. But in reality stock prices do not change continuously, as assumed by the normal distribution, or even, necessarily, by small increments. October 19, 1987, provided sobering evidence of this fact. Moreover, many investment strategies, especially those that involve options or dynamic trading rules, often generate return distributions that are significantly skewed, rather than symmetric. In these instances, the assumption of a normal distribution might result in significant errors in probability estimates.[5]

The normal distribution can be applied in a wide variety of circumstances to help financial analysts measure and control uncertainty associated with financial variables, but it is typically an inexact model of reality.

Notes

1. Such diverse phenomenon as noise in electromagnetic systems, the dynamics of star clustering, the eruption of Old Faithful, and the evolution of ecological systems behave in accordance with the predictions of a normal distribution.

2. To be precise, we should divide by the number of observations less one, because we lose one degree of freedom by using the same data to calculate the mean. This correction yields a so-called unbiased estimate of the variance, which typically is of little practical consequence.

3. For a more detailed discussion of the lognormal distribution, see Chapter 4.

4. The value of an option depends on the price of the underlying asset, the exercise price, the time to expiration, the risk-free return and the standard deviation of the underlying asset. All these values except the standard deviation are known, and the standard deviation can be inferred from the price at which the option trades. The implied value for the standard deviation is solved for iteratively. For a review of this technique, see Chapter 12.

5. For an excellent discussion of this issue, see R. Bookstaber and R. Clarke, "Problems in Evaluating the Performance of Portfolios with Options," *Financial Analysts Journal*, January/February 1985.

3
Utility

An important axiom of modern financial theory is that rational investors seek to maximize expected utility. Many financial analysts, however, find the concept of utility somewhat nebulous. This chapter discusses the origin of utility theory as well as its application within the context of financial analysis.

In his classic paper, "Exposition of a New Theory on the Measurement of Risk," first published in 1738, Daniel Bernoulli proposed the following: "the determination of the value of an item must not be based on its price, but rather on the utility it yields. The price of the item is dependent only on the thing itself and is equal for everyone; the utility, however, is dependent on the particular circumstances of the person making the estimate. Thus there is no doubt that a gain of one thousand ducats is more significant to a pauper than to a rich man though both gain the same amount."[1]

Bernoulli's insight that the utility of a gain depends on one's wealth may seem rather obvious and perhaps even pedestrian, yet it has profound implications for the theory of risk. Figure 3.1 helps us to visualize Bernoulli's notion of utility, which economists today call diminishing marginal utility.

The horizontal axis represents wealth, while the vertical axis represents utility. The relation between wealth and utility is measured by the curved line. Utility clearly increases with wealth, because the curve has a positive slope. The positive slope simply indicates that we prefer more wealth to less wealth. This assumption seldom invites dispute.

As wealth increases, the increments to utility become progressively smaller, as the concave shape of the curve reveals. This concavity indicates that we derive less and less satisfaction with each subsequent unit of incremental wealth. Technically, Bernoulli's notion of utility implies that its first derivative with respect to wealth is positive, while its second derivative is negative.

A negative second derivative implies that we would experience greater *dis*utility from a decline in wealth than the utility we would

Figure 3.1   Diminishing Marginal Utility

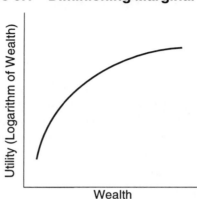

derive from an equal increase in wealth. This tradeoff is apparent in Figure 3.2, which shows the changes in utility associated with an equal increase and decrease in wealth.

According to Bernoulli, the precise change in utility associated with a change in wealth equals the logarithm of the sum of initial wealth plus the increment to wealth, divided by initial wealth. For example, the increase in utility associated with an increase in wealth from \$100 to \$150 equals 0.405465, as follows:

Figure 3.2   Changes in Utility versus Changes in Wealth

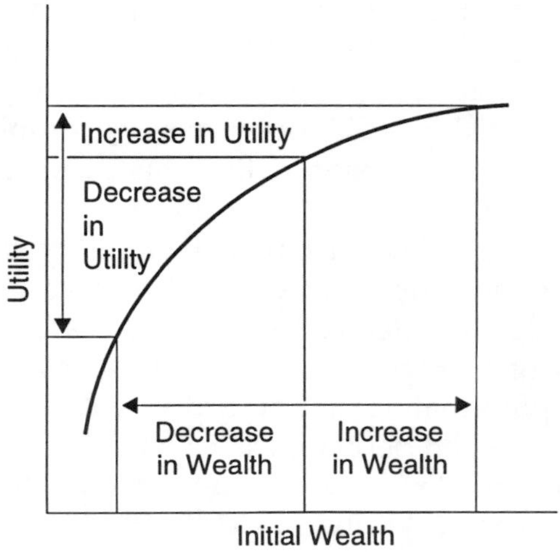

$$0.405465 = \ln\left(\frac{100 + 50}{100}\right)$$

The next \$50 increment to wealth, however, yields a smaller increment to utility:

$$0.287682 = \ln\left(\frac{150 + 50}{150}\right)$$

Risk Aversion

From Bernoulli's assumption of diminishing marginal utility, it follows that those whose utility is defined by the logarithm of wealth will reject a "fair game"—that is, a game in which the expected outcome is the same for each participant. Bernoulli offered the following example. Two participants, each of whom has \$100 (Bernoulli used ducats), contribute \$50 as a stake in a game in which the chance of winning is determined by the toss of a coin. Each player therefore has a 50 percent probability of ending up with \$50 and a 50 percent probability of ending up with \$150.

The expected value of this game is \$100 (0.5 · 50 + 0.5 · 150). This is identical to the expected value of not playing, because each participant starts out with \$100. The expected utility of this game, however, is found by adding the utility (logarithm) of the \$50 payoff times its probability of occurring to the utility of the \$150 payoff times its probability of occurring.

Table 3.1 shows the results. The utility of not participating in the game equals the logarithm of \$100 dollars, which is 4.61. The utility of not participating is higher than the utility of participating. Thus a player whose utility with respect to wealth is defined as the logarithm of wealth will reject the game, even though it is fair.

In essence, Bernoulli's concept of utility implies that we prefer a certain prospect to an uncertain prospect of equal value. That is to

Table 3.1 Expected Utility of Participating in Fair Game

Payoff	Utility of Payoff	Probability of Payoff	Probability-Weighted Payoff
50	3.91	50%	1.96
150	5.01	50%	2.50
Expected Utility			4.46

say, we are risk averse. In fact, Bernoulli interpreted risk aversion as "nature's admonition to avoid the dice."[2]

Certainty Equivalent

With simple algebra, we can extend Bernoulli's insight a little further and determine how much value we would be willing to subtract from a certain prospect before we would select a risky prospect. The value of the certain prospect that yields the same utility as the expected utility of an uncertain prospect is called the certainty equivalent.

We have already seen that the expected utility of a risky prospect is computed as the logarithm of the favorable outcome times its probability of occurring plus the logarithm of the unfavorable outcome times its probability of occurring (which would equal one minus the probability of occurrence of the favorable outcome). We can set this formula equal to the logarithm of the certain prospect and solve for the value of the certain prospect, as follows:

$$\ln(C) = \ln(F) \cdot p + \ln(U) \cdot (1-p)$$

$$C = e^{[\ln(F) \cdot p + \ln(U) \cdot (1-p)]}$$

where
  $\ln$ = natural logarithm,
  C = certain payoff,
  F = payoff from favorable outcome,
  U = payoff from unfavorable outcome,
  p = probability of occurrence for favorable outcome and
  e = 2.71828.

In Bernoulli's example, in which each participant has a 50 percent chance of receiving $150 and a 50 percent chance of receiving $50, the certainty equivalent is $86.60:

$$C = e^{[\ln(150) \cdot 0.5 + \ln(50) \cdot (1-0.5)]}$$

$$86.60 = e^{[2.5053 + 1.9560]}$$

The certainty equivalent of $86.60 implies that we would be indifferent between a certain $86.60 payoff and a risky prospect with an equal probability of paying $150 or $50. It follows that we would select the risky prospect only if it offered a higher expected value than the certain prospect. The difference in expected value that would induce us to choose the risky prospect is called the required risk premium.

We have thus far assumed that our initial wealth equals only $100. Assume, instead, that we were starting with initial wealth of $1,000 dollars, so that we would receive $1,050 given a favorable outcome and $950 given an unfavorable outcome. The certainty equivalent would then equal $998.75. Whereas a person with only $100 would demand a risk premium of more than 13 percent ([100 − 86.60]/100), a person with $1,000 would demand a risk premium of only one-eighth of 1 percent ([1,000 − 998.75]/1000). The wealthier person is still risk averse, but he is not nearly as disinclined as the poorer one to incur the risk of losing $50, because this amount represents but a small fraction of his wealth. Of course, if the potential gain or loss from the risky prospect was $500, he too would prefer a 13 percent risk premium.

It is easy to see how this framework also enables us to determine how much we should pay to insure against various risks. Suppose, for example, that we have $100,000 of savings and we inherit a family heirloom valued at $10,000, which is to be mailed to us. Suppose further that there is a 1 percent chance that the heirloom will be lost in the mail. Based on Bernoulli's model of risk aversion, we should be willing to pay up to $104.79 to insure this heirloom.

The total payoff, should the heirloom arrive safely, equals $110,000, which yields utility of 11.6082. If the heirloom is lost in the mail, the total payoff equals $100,000, which yields utility of 11.5129. Thus the expected utility of this risky prospect equals 11.6073 (11.6082 · 0.99 + 11.5129 · 0.01). This expected utility corresponds to a certainty equivalent of $109,895.21. Thus we should be willing to pay up to $104.79 (110,000 − 109,895.21) to insure the heirloom.

The Rhetoric of Risk Preference

Bernoulli's view of utility is certainly plausible, but we should not conclude that it describes everyone's attitude toward risk. Economists have generalized Bernoulli's insights into a comprehensive theory of risk preference accompanied by the usual classifications and rhetoric. For example, economists distinguish between those who are risk averse, those who are risk neutral and those who seek risk. A risk-averse person will reject a fair game, while a risk-neutral person will be indifferent to a fair game and a risk seeker will select a fair game. Economists also distinguish between the absolute amount of one's wealth that is exposed to risk versus the proportion of one's wealth that is exposed to risk, and whether this amount decreases, remains constant or increases as wealth increases.

Decreasing absolute risk aversion indicates that the amount of wealth one is willing to expose to risk increases as one's wealth increases. Constant absolute risk aversion implies that the amount of wealth exposed to risk remains unchanged as wealth increases. Increasing absolute risk aversion means that absolute risk exposure decreases as wealth increases.

Relative risk aversion refers to changes in the percentage of one's wealth exposed to risk as wealth increases. Decreasing relative risk aversion implies that the percentage of wealth exposed to risk increases as wealth increases. With constant relative risk aversion, the percentage of wealth exposed to risk does not change as wealth increases. Increasing relative risk aversion implies that percentage risk exposure decreases as wealth increases. Table 3.2 summarizes these relationships.

Indifference Curves

In many applications, it is convenient to model expected utility as a function of expected return and risk as measured by the standard deviation of returns. Because most investors are indeed risk averse, expected utility is usually depicted as a positive function of expected return and a negative function of risk:[3]

$$E(U) = E(r) - \lambda \cdot \sigma^2$$

where
$E(U)$ = expected utility,
$E(r)$ = expected return,
σ = standard deviation of returns *and*
λ = risk-aversion coefficient.

Table 3.2 Risk Aversion

	Absolute	Relative
Decreasing	Increase Risky Amount	Increase Risky Percentage
Constant	Maintain Risky Amount	Maintain Risky Percentage
Increasing	Decrease Risky Amount	Decrease Risky Percentage

The risk-aversion coefficient has no economic meaning in and of itself. It is merely an index of our aversion toward risk. Of course, if we are risk averse, the coefficient must be positive. And the higher the value of the coefficient, the more risk averse we would be.

Suppose, for example, that our risk-aversion coefficient equals 5. An asset with an expected return of 8 percent and a standard deviation of 10 percent would yield expected utility of 3.0 percent. Another asset may have an expected return of 10 percent and a standard deviation of 12 percent. The expected utility from this asset, given our aversion toward risk, would equal 2.8 percent. The return of the second asset is not high enough to compensate for its higher risk, even though its expected return and risk are both 2 percent higher than those of the first asset. Given a risk-aversion coefficient equal to 5, we would prefer the less risky asset.

If we were less risk averse, with a coefficient of 3, say, the first asset would yield expected utility of 5.0 percent, while the second asset would yield expected utility of 5.7 percent. In this case, the incremental expected return of the second asset is sufficient to counter its higher risk. Table 3.3 summarizes these results.

It is possible to identify combinations of expected return and standard deviation that yield the same level of expected utility for a particular risk-aversion coefficient. Table 3.4 shows several combinations based on a risk-aversion coefficient of 4. It indicates that we are more inclined to incur risk in order to increase expected return at low levels of expected return than we are at higher levels of expected return.

Table 3.3 The Risk-Aversion Coefficient

	Coefficient = 5			
	Expected Return	Standard Deviation	Expected Utility	Preference
Asset 1	8.0%	10.0%	3.0%	←
Asset 2	10.0%	12.0%	2.8%	

	Coefficient = 3			
	Expected Return	Standard Deviation	Expected Utility	Preference
Asset 1	8.0%	10.0%	5.0%	
Asset 2	10.0%	12.0%	5.7%	←

For example, if we are starting from an expected return of 5 percent, we are willing to accept five additional units of risk in order to increase our expected return by one unit. If, however, we are starting from an expected return of 15 percent, we are willing to accept only 0.77 units of incremental risk in order to gain one additional unit of expected return.

Tracing a curve through all the combinations of expected return and risk with equal expected utility creates an indifference curve. Figure 3.3 shows three hypothetical indifference curves. Indifference curves that are closer to the upper left corner yield more expected utility and thus are more desirable. Given a particular indifference curve, however, all the points along that curve yield the same expected utility.

If we were to combine a set of risky assets efficiently so that for any given level of expected return we minimized risk, a continuum of such combinations would form a concave curve in dimensions of expected return and risk. Figure 3.4 shows such a curve, which is called the efficient frontier, along with three indifference curves.[4] The

Table 3.4 Risk-Return Combinations with Equal Utility
(risk aversion coefficient = 4)

Expected Return	Standard Deviation	Expected Utility
5.00	0.00	5.00
6.00	5.00	5.00
7.00	7.07	5.00
8.00	8.66	5.00
9.00	10.00	5.00
10.00	11.18	5.00
11.00	12.25	5.00
12.00	13.23	5.00
13.00	14.14	5.00
14.00	15.00	5.00
15.00	15.81	5.00
16.00	16.58	5.00
17.00	17.32	5.00
18.00	18.03	5.00
19.00	18.71	5.00
20.00	19.56	5.00

Figure 3.3 Indifference Curves

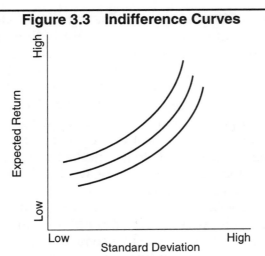

point of tangency between the efficient frontier and indifference curve 2 represents the precise combination of expected return and standard deviation that maximizes expected utility. It matches our preference for incurring risk in order to raise expected return with the best available tradeoff of risk and return from the capital markets.

Figure 3.4 The Optimal Portfolio

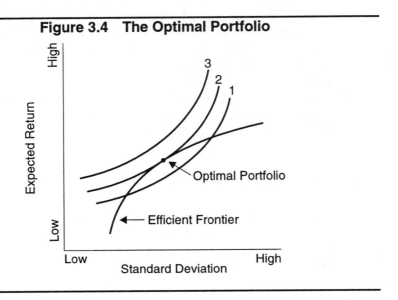

Clearly, we would prefer a combination of expected return and risk located along indifference curve 3, but indifference curve 3 is located in a region that is unobtainable. Indifference curve 1, on the other hand, is undesirable because it is dominated by many of the combinations along the efficient frontier. This illustration shows how we can employ utility theory to identify a portfolio of assets that is optimal given our particular attitude toward risk.

The concept of utility is critical to the theory of choice under uncertainty. While it is reasonable to accept the basic premises of utility theory, such as the notion that more wealth is preferred to less wealth and that investors are typically risk averse, it is important to recognize that concise mathematical models of utility may not always reflect the full range of investor attitudes and idiosyncrasies. We should be sensitive to the fact that some descriptions of utility are put forth primarily for tractability or expository convenience.[5]

Notes

1. D. Bernoulli, "Exposition of a New Theory on the Measurement of Risk," *Econometrica*, January 1954 (translation from 1738 version). Daniel Bernoulli is one of several celebrated Bernoulli mathematicians. Daniel's father, Johann, made important contributions to calculus, although much of his work was published by the Marquis de l'Hospital. Johann was also the mentor of the famous prodigy Leonhard Euler. The most renowned Bernoulli was Daniel's uncle and Johann's older brother Jakob. Jakob Bernoulli is known primarily for his contributions to the theory of probability. Finally, Daniel's cousin, Nicolas Bernoulli, was a distinguished mathematician who proposed the famous St. Petersburg Paradox, for which Daniel offered a solution in his classic risk measurement paper.

2. Ibid., p. 29.

3. The capital markets offer compelling evidence of risk aversion. Historically, investors have priced assets to extract a premium for bearing risk; to wit, annually from 1926 through 1991, stocks have returned 5.6 percent more than government bonds, and government bonds have returned 1.1 percent more than Treasury bills.

4. For a more detailed discussion of the efficient frontier, see Chapter 1.

5. For a basic review of utility theory, see E. Elton and M. Gruber, *Modern Portfolio Theory and Investment Analysis*, third edition (New York: John Wiley & Sons, 1987), pp. 179–203. For a more technical discussion of utility theory, see C. Huang and R. Litzenberger, Foundations for Financial Economics (New York: North-Holland, 1988), pp. 1–37.

4
Lognormality

When reading the financial literature we often see statements to the effect that a particular result depends on the assumption that returns are *lognormally* distributed. What exactly is a lognormal distribution, and why is it relevant to financial analysis? In order to address this question, let us start with a review of logarithms.

Logarithms

A logarithm is simply the power to which a base must be raised to yield a particular value. For example, the exponent 2 is the logarithm of 16 to the base 4, because 4 squared equals 16. The logarithm of 8 to the base 4 equals 1.5, because 4 raised to the power 1.5 equals 8.

The choice of a base depends on the context in which we use logarithms. For simple mathematical procedures, it is common to use the base 10, which explains why logarithms to the base 10 are called common logs. The base 10 is popular because the logarithms of 10, 100, 1000 and so on equal 1, 2, 3, ..., respectively.

Why should we care about logarithms? In the days prior to pocket calculators (long before my time), logarithms were useful for performing complicated computations. Financial analysts would multiply large numbers by summing their logarithms, and they would divide them by subtracting their logarithms. For example, given a base of 4, we can multiply 16 times 8 by raising the number 4 to the 3.5 power, which is the sum of the logarithms 2 and 1.5. Of course, you might argue that it would have been easier to multiply large numbers directly than to raise a base to a fractional power. In the olden days, however, an analyst would use a slide rule, which is a ruler with a sliding central strip marked with logarithmic scales.

e

In most financial applications, instead of logarithms to the base 10, we use logarithms to the base 2.71828, which is denoted by the letter e. These logarithms, which are called natural logs and are abbreviated as ln, have a special property. Suppose we invest $100 at the beginning of the year at an annual interest rate of 100 percent. At the end of the year we will receive $200—our original principal of $100 and another $100 of interest. Now suppose our interest is compounded semiannually. Our year-end payment will equal $225. By the middle of the year we will have earned $50 of interest, which is then reinvested to generate the additional $25.

In general, we can use the following formula to compute the year-end value of our investment for any interest rate and for any frequency of compounding:

$$E = B \cdot (1 + r/n)^n$$

where
  E = ending value,
  B = beginning investment,
  r = annual interest rate and
  n = frequency of compounding.

If the 100 percent rate of interest is compounded quarterly, our $100 investment will grow to $244.14 by the end of the year. If it is compounded daily, we will receive $271.46. And if it is compounded hourly, we will receive $271.81 by year-end.

It seems as though the more frequently our interest is compounded, the more money we will end up with at the end of the year. No matter how frequently it is compounded, though, we will never receive more than $271.83. When r equals 100 percent, the limit of the function $(1 + r/n)^n$ as n approaches infinity is 2.71828, the base of the natural log.

We can use this result to convert periodic rates of return into continuous rates of return. A periodic rate of return is computed as the percentage change of our investment from the beginning of the period to the end of the period, assuming there are no contributions or disbursements. A continuous rate of return assumes that the income and growth are compounded instantaneously.

From our previous example we know that e, the base of the natural log, raised to the power 1 (the continuous rate of return in our example) yields 1 plus 171.83 percent (the periodic rate of return in our example). The natural log of the quantity 1 plus the periodic rate of return must therefore equal the corresponding continuous rate of return. For example, the natural log of the quantity 1 plus 10 percent equals 9.53 percent. This means that if we invest $100 at a continuously compounded rate of return of 9.53 percent, our investment will grow to $110. The value 1.10, which we compute by raising e to the power 0.0953, is called the exponential. These relationships are shown below:

$$\ln(1.10) = 0.0953,$$

$$1.10 = 2.71828^{0.0953}$$

We can also compute the continuous rate of return within a period by subtracting the natural log of the beginning value from the natural log of the ending value. Suppose we start with $100, which is invested so that it grows to $150 after one year, $225 after two years and $337.50 after three years. The logarithms of these values equal 4.6052, 5.0106, 5.4161 and 5.8216, respectively. The difference between each logarithm and the next one equals the continuously compounded return each year, which is 40.55 percent. This continuous return corresponds to a yearly periodic return of 50 percent.

If we plot these values as a function of time, we produce a convex curve, as shown in Figure 4.1. The logarithms of these values, however, form a straight line when plotted as a function of time, indicating a constant periodic rate of growth. It is this relation that gives rise to the logarithmic scale, in which equal percentage changes corre-

Figure 4.1   Continuously Compounded Return as a Function of Time

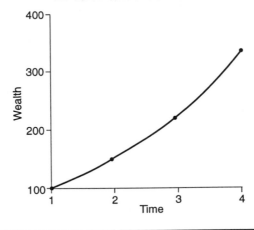

spond to equal vertical distances. This scale is shown on the left axis in Figure 4.2, with the logarithms shown along the right axis.

Why Are Returns Lognormally Distributed?

Suppose we invest $100 for one year and suppose that the quarterly returns during this period are 10 percent, –5 percent, 15 percent, and –10 percent. Although the sum of these quarterly returns equals 10 percent, our $100 investment grows, not to $110, but to $108.16 ($100 · 1.10 · 0.95 · 1.15 · 0.90), yielding a one-year cumulative return of 8.16 percent. The sum of the quarterly returns does not measure the actual cumulative return we realize. It is the compounding of these quarterly returns that yields the cumulative return.

We can sum the natural logs of the quantities 1 plus the quarterly returns to determine the cumulative return. These natural logs equal 0.0953, –0.0513, 0.1398, and –0.1054, respectively, and they sum to 0.0784. If we raise e to the power 0.0784, we get the exponential 1.0816, which equals 1 plus the one-year cumulative rate of return.

What has all this to do with lognormality? We have seen that the sum of the logarithms of the quantities 1 plus the periodic returns equals the logarithm of the quantity 1 plus the cumulative return. The important distinction is that we sum the natural logs to derive the cumulative return, whereas we multiply 1 plus the periodic returns to derive the cumulative return.

Figure 4.2 Logarithms of Returns
as a Function of Time

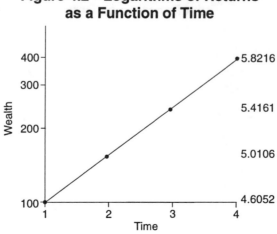

The Central Limit Theorem, which is one of the most important notions of statistical inference, deals with the summation of random variables. A normal distribution, which is symmetric, can be described by its first two moments—its mean and its variance.[1] Skewness has a value of 0 in a normal distribution because it is computed by raising a value to an odd-number exponent; unlike variance, which is computed by squaring a value, skewness can take on either a positive or a negative value. When a large number of random variables are summed, the higher moments that are computed with odd-number exponents tend to cancel each other out.

Because we sum logarithms, the natural logs of the quantities 1 plus the periodic returns are normally distributed. Because these natural logs are normally distributed, and because the exponential of the normal distribution gives the lognormal distribution, the quantities 1 plus the periodic returns, which are the exponentials of the natural logs, are lognormally distributed.

Normal Distribution and Lognormal Distribution

Having said all that, why should we care? Table 4.1 shows the estimated probabilities of achieving various annualized holding-period returns for an investment with a mean return of 12.3 percent, a geometric return of 10.5 percent, a standard deviation of periodic returns equal to 20 percent, and a standard deviation of the logarithms of 1 plus the periodic returns equal to 18 percent.

Given a one-year horizon, it does not make very much difference whether we assume a normal distribution or a lognormal distribution to estimate probabilities.[2] As we extend our horizon, however, the normal distribution overestimates the probability of achieving target returns that are below the expected return. For example, given a

Table 4.1 Probability of Achieving Target Returns

Target Returns	One Year		Five Years		10 Years	
	N	L	N	L	N	L
–5%	81%	80%	99%	97%	100%	100%
0	73	71	96	89	100	96
8	59	55	76	61	95	66
20	35	32	6	15	0	7

five-year horizon, the likelihood of achieving at least an 8 percent annualized return equals 76 percent, assuming a normal distribution, versus 61 percent for a lognormal distribution. Over 10 years, the difference is even greater. Based on a normal distribution, there is a 95 percent chance of achieving at least an 8 percent return, while under the assumption of a lognormal distribution, the probability falls to 66 percent. The normal distribution also *under*estimates the probability of achieving target returns above the expected return. Given a five-year horizon and assuming a normal distribution, the chance of achieving a return of 20 percent or greater equals 6 percent, versus 15 percent for a lognormal distribution. Over a 10-year horizon, the probabilities equal 0 percent and 7 percent for the normal and lognormal distributions, respectively.

Based on this evidence, we are well advised to note whether a normal or lognormal distribution was assumed in generating the results of interest to us, especially if they pertain to a multiyear horizon.

Notes

1. For a review of the normal distribution, see Chapter 2.

2. The normal deviate for the normal distribution is computed as:

$$\frac{[(1 + T)^n - (1 + R)^n]}{(\sigma \cdot \sqrt{n})}$$

where
  T = target return,
  R = mean of periodic returns,
  σ = standard deviation of periodic returns and
  n = number of years.

The normal deviate for the lognormal distribution is computed as:

$$\frac{[\ln(1 + T) \cdot n - \ln(1 + R^*) \cdot n]}{(\sigma \cdot \sqrt{n})}$$

where
  R^* = geometric return and
  σ^* = standard deviations of logarithms of one plus periodic returns.

5
Return and Risk

At first glance, return and risk may seem to be straightforward concepts. Yet closer inspection reveals nuances that can have important consequences for determining the appropriate method for evaluating financial results. This chapter reviews various measures of return and risk with an emphasis on their suitability for alternative uses.

Return

Perhaps the most straightforward rate of return is the *holding-period return* (HPR). It equals the income generated by an investment plus the investment's change in price during the period the investment is held, all divided by the beginning price. For example, if we purchased a share of common stock for $50.00, received a $2.00 dividend, and sold the stock for $55.00, we would have achieved a holding-period return equal to 14 percent. In general, we can use Equation (1) to compute holding-period returns.

$$HPR = (I + E - B)/B \qquad (1)$$

where
HPR = holding-period return,
   I = income,
   E = ending price and
   B = beginning price.

Holding-period returns are also referred to as *periodic returns.*

Dollar-Weighted versus Time-Weighted Rates of Return

Now let us consider rates of return over multiple holding periods. Suppose that a mutual fund generated the following annual holding-period returns from 1988 through 1992:

1988	−5.00%
1989	−15.20%
1990	3.10%
1991	30.75%
1992	17.65%

Suppose further that we had invested $75,000 in this fund by making contributions at the beginning of each year according to the following schedule:

1988	$ 5,000
1989	$10,000
1990	$15,000
1991	$20,000
1992	$25,000

By the end of 1992, our investment would have grown in value to $103,804.56. By discounting the ending value of our investment and the interim cash flows back to our initial contribution, we can determine the investment's *dollar-weighted rate of return* (DWR), which is also referred to as the *internal rate of return:*

$$5,000 = -\frac{10,000}{(1+r)} - \frac{15,000}{(1+r)^2} - \frac{20,000}{(1+r)^3} - \frac{25,000}{(1+r)^4} + \frac{103,805}{(1+r)^5}$$

DWR = 14.25%

We enter the interim contributions as negative values, because they are analogous to negative dividend payments. Although we cannot solve directly for the dollar-weighted rate of return, most financial calculators and spreadsheet software have iterative algorithms that quickly converge to a solution. In our example, the solution equals 14.25 percent.

The dollar-weighted rate of return measures the annual rate at which our cumulative contributions grow over the measurement period. However, it is not a reliable measure of the performance of the mutual fund in which we invested, because it depends on the timing of the cash flows. Suppose, for example, we reversed the order of the contributions. Given this sequence of contributions, our investment would have grown to a higher value—$103,893.76. The dollar-weighted rate of return, however, would have been only 9.12 percent:

$$25,000 = -\frac{20,000}{(1+r)} - \frac{15,000}{(1+r)^2} - \frac{10,000}{(1+r)^3} - \frac{5,000}{(1+r)^4} + \frac{103,894}{(1+r)^5}$$

DWR = 9.12%

In order to measure the underlying performance of the mutual fund, we can calculate its *time-weighted rate of return*. This measure does not depend on the timing of cash flows.

We compute the time-weighted rate of return by first adding one to each year's holding-period return to determine the return's *wealth relative*. Then we multiply the wealth relatives together, raise the product to the power 1 divided by the number of years in the measurement period, and subtract 1. Equation (2) shows this calculation:

$$\text{TWR} = \left[\prod_{i=1}^{n} (1 + \text{HPR}_i) \right]^{1/n} - 1 \qquad (2)$$

where
TWR = time-weighted rate of return,
HPR_i = holding-period return for year i and
n = number of years in measurement period.

If we substitute the mutual fund's holding-period returns into equation (2), we discover that the fund's time-weighted rate of return equals 5.02 percent.

The time-weighted rate of return is also called the *geometric return* or the *compound annual return*. Although the geometric return and the compound annual return are often used interchangeably, technically the geometric return pertains to a population whereas the compound annual return pertains to a sample. I use the term geometric return to refer to both. It is the rate of return that, when compounded annually, determines the ending value of our initial investment assuming there are no interim cash flows. For example, suppose we invest $10,000 in a strategy that produces a holding-period rate of return of 50 percent in the first year and –50 percent in the second year. At the end of the second year, we will end up with $7,500. The geometric return over the two-year measurement period equals – 13.40 percent:

$$[(1 + 0.5)(1 - 0.5)]^{1/2} - 1 = -0.1340$$

If we multiply $10,000 × (1 − 0.1340) and then multiply this result again by (1 − 0.1340), we arrive at the ending value of this investment—$7500.

In order to manipulate geometric returns, we must first convert them to wealth relatives and raise the wealth relatives to a power equal to the number of years in the measurement period. Then we multiply or divide the cumulative wealth relatives, annualize the result, and subtract one in order to convert the result back into a geometric return.

Suppose, for example, that five years ago we invested $100,000 in a fund that we thought would earn a geometric return of 8 percent over a 20-year horizon so that at the end of the horizon we would receive $466,095.71. During the past five years, however, the fund's geometric return was only 6.50 percent. What must its geometric return be for the next 15 years if we are to reach our original goal of $466,095.71? We start by raising 1.08 to the 20th power, which equals 4.6609571. This value equals the cumulative wealth relative of the anticipated geometric return. We then raise the wealth relative of the geometric return realized thus far to the 5th power, which equals 1.3700867. We then divide 4.6609571 by 1.3700867, raise this value to the power 1 over 15, and subtract 1, to arrive at 8.50 percent.

Alternatively, we can convert wealth relatives to continuous returns by taking their natural logarithms and manipulating these logarithms. For example, the natural logarithm of 1.08 equals 0.076961, and the natural logarithm of 1.065 equals 0.062975. We multiply 0.062975 × 5 and subtract it from 0.076961 × 20, which equals 1.2243468. Then we divide this value by 15 and use the base of the natural logarithm 2.718281 to reconvert it to an annual wealth relative, which equals 1.085.[1]

Geometric Return versus Arithmetic Return

It is easy to see why the geometric return is a better description of past performance than the arithmetic average. In the example in which we invested $10,000 at a return of 50 percent followed by a return of −50 percent, the arithmetic average overstates the return on our investment. It did not grow at a constant rate of 0 percent, but declined by 13.40 percent compounded annually for two years. The arithmetic average will exceed the geometric average except when all the holding-period returns are the same; the two return measures will be the same in that case. Furthermore, the difference between the two averages will increase as the variability of the holding-period returns increases.

If we accept the past as prologue, which average should we use to estimate a future year's expected return? The best estimate of a future year's return based on a random distribution of the prior years' returns is the arithmetic average. Statistically, it is our best guess for the holding-period return in a given year. If we wish to estimate the expected value of an investment over a multiyear horizon conditioned on past experience, we should also use the arithmetic average. If, however, we wish to estimate the probability distribution of terminal wealth, we should use the geometric average.

Suppose we plan to invest $100,000 in an S&P 500 index fund, and we wish to estimate the median value of our investment five years from now. We assume there are no transaction costs or fees, and we base our estimates on yearly results ending December 31, 1992, which are shown in Table 5.1. The arithmetic average equals 16.83 percent, while the geometric average equals 16.20 percent. Our best estimate for next year's return, or any single year's return for that matter, equals 16.83 percent, because there is a 1-in-10 chance of experiencing each of the observed returns. However, the best estimate for the median value of our fund is based on the geometric average. It equals $211,866.94, which we derive by raising 1.1620 to the 5th power and multiplying this value by $100,000.

Risk

Although the time-weighted rate of return measures the constant annual rate of growth that determines terminal wealth, it is nonetheless limited as a measure of performance because it fails to account for risk. We can adjust returns for risk in several ways. One approach

Table 5.1 Annual S&P 500 Returns			
1983	22.63%	1988	16.58%
1984	5.86	1989	31.63
1985	31.61	1990	−3.14
1986	18.96	1991	31.56
1987	5.23	1992	7.33

is to compute a portfolio's return in excess of the riskless return and to divide this excess return by the portfolio's standard deviation. This risk-adjusted return, called the *Sharpe measure,* is given by equation (3).[2]

$$S = \frac{(R_p - R_F)}{\sigma_p} \tag{3}$$

where
  S = the Sharpe measure,
  R_p = portfolio return,
  R_F = riskless return and
  σ_p = the standard deviation of portfolio returns.

Because it adjusts return based on total portfolio risk, the implicit assumption of the Sharpe measure is that the portfolio will not be combined with other risky portfolios. Thus the Sharpe measure is relevant for performance evaluation when we wish to evaluate several mutually exclusive portfolios.

The Capital Asset Pricing Model (CAPM) assumes that risk consists of a systematic component and a specific component. Risk that is specific to individual securities can be diversified away, hence an investor should not expect compensation for bearing this type of risk. Therefore, when a portfolio is evaluated in combination with other portfolios, its excess return should be adjusted by its systematic risk rather than its total risk.[3]

The *Treynor measure* adjusts excess return for systematic risk.[4] It is computed by dividing a portfolio's excess return, not by its standard deviation, but by its beta, as shown in equation (4).

$$T = \frac{(R_p - R_F)}{\beta_p} \tag{4}$$

where
  T = the Treynor measure,
  R_p = portfolio return,
  R_F = riskless return and
  β_p = portfolio beta.

We can estimate beta by regressing a portfolio's excess returns on an appropriate benchmark's excess returns. Beta is the coefficient from such a regression. The Treynor measure is a valid performance criterion when we wish to evaluate a portfolio in combination with the benchmark portfolio and other actively managed portfolios.

The intercept from a regression of the portfolio's excess returns on the benchmark's excess returns is called *alpha*. Alpha measures the value-added of the portfolio, given its level of systematic risk. Alpha is referred to as the *Jensen measure,* and is given by equation (5).[5]

$$\alpha = (R_p - R_F) - \beta_p(R_B - R_F) \tag{5}$$

where
   α = the Jensen measure (alpha),
   R_p = portfolio return,
   R_F = riskless return,
   β_p = portfolio beta and
   R_B = benchmark return.

The Jensen measure is also suitable for evaluating a portfolio's performance in combination with other portfolios, because it is based on systematic risk rather than total risk.

If we wish to determine whether or not an observed alpha is due to skill or chance, we can compute an *appraisal ratio* by dividing alpha by the standard error of the regression:

$$A = \frac{\alpha}{\sigma_c} \tag{6}$$

where
   A = the appraisal ratio,
   α = alpha and
   σ_c = the standard error of the regression (nonsystematic risk).

The appraisal ratio compares alpha, the average nonsystematic deviation from the benchmark, with the nonsystematic risk incurred to generate this performance. In order to estimate the likelihood that an observed alpha is not due to chance, we can test the null hypothesis that the mean alpha does not differ significantly from 0 percent. If we reject the null hypothesis, the alpha is not due to chance.

Suppose, for example, that a portfolio's alpha equals 4 percent and that its standard error equals 3 percent, so that the appraisal ratio equals 1.33. If we look up this number in a t distribution table, we discover that, given the amount of nonsystematic risk, there is a 10 percent chance of observing an alpha of this magnitude by random process. Hence, we would fail to reject the null hypothesis that alpha does not differ significantly from 0 percent if we require 95% confidence.

Downside Risk

In the previous example, we based the probability estimate on the assumption that alpha is normally distributed. This assumption is reasonable for evaluating returns over short measurement periods. Over multiyear measurement periods, however, it is the logarithms of the wealth relatives that are normally distributed. The returns themselves are lognormally distributed, which means that they are positively skewed. Therefore, in order to estimate the likelihood of experiencing particular outcomes over multiyear horizons, we should calculate the normal deviate based on the mean and standard deviation of the logarithms of the wealth relatives.

Some investment strategies produce distributions that are skewed differently from a lognormal distribution. Dynamic trading strategies such as portfolio insurance or strategies that involve the use of options typically generate skewed distributions.

A distribution that is positively (right) skewed has a long tail above the mean. Although most of the outcomes are below the mean, they are of smaller magnitude than the fewer outcomes that are above the mean. A distribution that is negatively (left) skewed has a long tail below the mean. It has more outcomes above the mean, but they are smaller in magnitude than those below the mean.

Skewness is calculated as the sum of the probability-weighted cubed deviations around the mean. Risk-averse investors prefer positive skewness, because there is less chance of large negative deviations.

When we are evaluating strategies that have skewed distributions other than lognormal, we cannot rely on only return and standard deviation to estimate the likelihood of achieving a particular result. Nor can we compare portfolios or strategies that have different degrees of skewness using only these two characteristics. Instead, we can specify a target return and base our evaluation on the dispersion of returns below this target, rather than the dispersion of returns around the mean.[6] An alternative method for dealing with skewness is to define utility as a function of mean, variance and skewness and then to evaluate portfolios and strategies based on their expected utilities.

I have attempted to shed some light on the subtleties that distinguish various measures of return and risk. When we rely on these summary statistics to evaluate past results or to predict future consequences, it is important that we understand their precise meaning.

Notes

1. For a review of logarithms and continuous returns, see Chapter 4.

2. See W. Sharpe, "Mutual Fund Performance," *Journal of Business*, January 1966.

3. For a discussion of the Capital Asset Pricing Model, see Chapter 1.

4. See J. Treynor, "How to Rate Management of Investment Funds," *Harvard Business Review*, January-February 1965.

5. See M. Jensen, "The Performance of Mutual Funds in the Period 1945-1964," *Journal of Finance*, May 1968.

6. See W. V. Harlow, "Asset Allocation in a Downside-Risk Framework," *Financial Analysts Journal*, September/October 1991.

6
Duration and Convexity

In 1938, Frederick Macaulay published his classic book, *Some Theoretical Problems Suggested by the Movements of Interest Rates, Bond Yields and Stock Prices in the United States Since 1865.*[1] Although Macaulay focused primarily on the theory of interest rates, as an aside he introduced the concept of duration as a more precise alternative to maturity for measuring the life of a bond. As with many of the important innovations in finance, the investment community was slow to appreciate Macaulay's discovery of duration. It was not until the 1970s that professional investors began to substitute duration for maturity in order to measure a fixed income portfolio's exposure to interest rate risk.[2] Today, duration and convexity—the extent to which duration changes as interest rates change—are indispensable tools for fixed income investors. In this chapter, I review these important concepts and show how they are applied to manage interest rate risk.

Macaulay's Duration

A bond's maturity measures the time to receipt of the final principal repayment and, therefore, the length of time the bondholder is exposed to the risk that interest rates will increase and devalue the remaining cash flows. Although it is typically the case that, the longer a bond's maturity, the more sensitive its price is to changes in interest rates, this relationship does not always hold. Maturity is an inadequate measure of the sensitivity of a bond's price to changes in interest rates, because it ignores the effects of coupon payments and prepayment of principal.

Consider two bonds, both of which mature in 10 years. Suppose the first bond is a zero-coupon bond that pays $2,000 at maturity, while the second bond pays a coupon of $100 annually and $1,000 at maturity. Although both bonds yield the same total cash flow, the bondholder must wait 10 years to receive the cash flow from the zero-coupon bond, while he receives almost half the cash flow from the coupon-bearing bond prior to its maturity. Therefore, the average time to receipt of the cash flow of the coupon-bearing bond is significantly shorter than it is for the zero-coupon bond.

The first cash flow from the coupon-bearing bond comes after one year, the second after two years, and so on. On average, the bondholder receives the cash flow in 5.5 years $((1 + 2 + 3 + \ldots + 10)/10)$. In the case of the zero-coupon bond, the bondholder receives a single cash flow after 10 years.

This computation of the average time to receipt of cash flows is an inadequate measure of the effective life of a bond, because it fails to account for the relative magnitudes of the cash flows. The principal repayment of the coupon-bearing bond is 10 times the size of each of the coupon payments. It makes sense to weight the time to receipt of the principal repayment more heavily than the times to receipt of the coupon payments.

Suppose we weight it 10 times as heavily as each coupon payment and compute the weighted average of these values. This approach yields a weighted average time to receipt of 7.75 years. But this measure too is deficient because it ignores the time value of money. A $100 coupon payment to be received two years from today is less valuable than a $100 coupon payment to be received one year hence.

Macaulay recognized this distinction and determined that the time to receipt of each cash flow should be weighted not by the relative magnitude of the cash flow but by the present value of its relative magnitude. Macaulay's duration, therefore, equals the average time to receipt of a bond's cash flows, in which each cash flow's time to receipt is weighted by its present value as a percentage of the total present value of all the cash flows. The sum of the present values of all the cash flows, of course, equals the price of the bond.

Assume that the yield to maturity of a 10-year bond equals 10 percent. The duration of the zero-coupon bond maturing in 10 years is the same as its maturity, because the time to receipt of the principal repayment is weighted 100 percent. The duration of the coupon-paying bond, though, is significantly shorter. It is not, however, as short as 5.5 years, the average time to receipt of the cash flow ignoring the relative sizes of the payments. Nor is it as long as 7.75 years, the estimate that accounts for the relative sizes of the cash flows but ignores their present values. The duration of the coupon-bearing bond equals 6.76 years, as Table 6.1 shows.

Table 6.1 Macaulay's Duration (yield to maturity = 10%)

Cash Flow	Time to Receipt (years)	Present Value of Cash Flow	Weight	Weighted-Value Time to Receipt
100	1	90.91	0.0909	0.0909
100	2	82.64	0.0826	0.1653
100	3	75.13	0.0751	0.2254
100	4	68.30	0.0683	0.2732
100	5	62.09	0.0621	0.3105
100	6	56.45	0.0565	0.3387
100	7	51.32	0.0513	0.3592
100	8	46.65	0.0467	0.3732
100	9	42.41	0.0424	0.3817
1,100	10	424.10	0.4241	4.2410
2,000	55	1,000.00	1.0000	6.7591

In general, we can write the formula for Macaulay's duration as follows:

$$D = \frac{\displaystyle\sum_{t=1}^{n} \frac{t \cdot C_t}{(1+y)^t}}{\displaystyle\sum_{t=1}^{n} \frac{C_t}{(1+y)^t}}$$

where
   D = duration,
   n = number of cash flows,
   t = time to receipt of the cash flow,
   C = cash flow amount and
   y = yield to maturity.

Properties of Duration

It is apparent from the formula for Macaulay's duration that its value depends on three factors—the final maturity of the bond, the coupon payments and the yield to maturity.

If we hold constant the size of the coupon payments and the yield to maturity, duration in general increases with a bond's maturity. But it increases at a slower rate than the increase in maturity, because later cash flows are discounted more heavily than earlier cash flows. If we extend the maturity of the coupon-bearing bond described earlier from 10 years to 15 years, for example, its duration increases by only 1.61 years, from 6.76 years to 8.37 years. Of course, in the case of zero-coupon bonds, duration increases exactly with maturity, because these values are equal to each other.

Deep-discount bonds are another exception to the general rule. They increase in duration as maturity increases up to a distant threshold and then decrease in duration as maturity increases beyond this threshold. This peculiar result arises because deep-discount bonds with sufficiently long maturities behave like perpetuities (bonds that pay coupons forever). Perpetuities have an infinite maturity but a finite duration, because the weight of the principal repayment is inconsequential by the time it is discounted to present value.

At a given maturity and yield to maturity, duration declines with increases in the coupon payments or principal prepayments. This is because a larger percentage of the total cash flow is received earlier; stated differently, the times to receipt of the coupon payments or principal prepayments are weighted more heavily relative to the final repayment of principal. If the coupon payments from our earlier example were $120 rather than $100, the bond's duration would equal 6.54 years instead of 6.76 years.

Finally, if we increase yield to maturity while holding the coupon payments and maturity constant, duration will fall, because the discount factors for the later cash flows increase more than the discount factors for the earlier cash flows. The duration of the coupon-bearing bond in our example, for instance, declines to 6.55 years as the yield to maturity rises to 12 percent. Table 6.2 summarizes these properties of duration.

Table 6.2 Properties of Duration

Maturity Increases:	Duration Increases[*]
Coupon Payment Increases:	Duration Decreases
Yield to Maturity Increases:	Duration Decreases

[*] For par and premium bonds. For deep-discount bonds, duration increases up to a distant threshold and then decreases.

Modified Duration

Although Macaulay conceived of duration as a measure of the effective life of a bond, it can be modified to measure the sensitivity of a bond's price to changes in the yield to maturity. The modification simply requires dividing Macaulay's duration by the quantity 1 plus the yield to maturity, as shown below:[3]

$$D_m = \frac{D}{(1 + y)}$$

where
  D_m = modified duration,
  D = Macaulay's duration and
  y = yield to maturity.

We can estimate the percentage change in the price of a bond by multiplying the basis-point change in yield to maturity by –1 times the bond's modified duration. Again, suppose that we have a 10-year bond that pays a $100 coupon annually and $1,000 at maturity; its yield to maturity is 10 percent. The Macaulay duration of this bond equals 6.76 years. Its modified duration thus equals 6.14 years, which we derive by dividing 6.76 by 1.10.

If yield to maturity increases 10 basis points to 10.1 percent, modified duration predicts that the bond's price will decline 0.614 percent, to $993.86. And if yield to maturity declines 10 basis points to 9.90 percent, modified duration predicts that the bond's price will increase 0.614 percent, to $1,006.14.

Although these predictions are close to the true answer, they are not exact. If yield to maturity does increase by 10 basis points, the price of the bond will actually decline by 0.612 percent, to $993.88, and if yield to maturity falls 10 basis points, the bond's price will increase by 0.617 percent, to $1,006.17. Modified duration apparently overestimates price declines and underestimates price increases with respect to changes in yield to maturity.

One might argue that the errors are so tiny as to be inconsequential. For larger changes in yield to maturity, however, the percentage change in price predicted by modified duration can be significantly wrong. For example, modified duration predicts a 6.14 percent change in price for a 100-basis-point change in yield to maturity, given our particular example. In fact, the bond's price would decline by only 5.89 percent if yield to maturity rose by 100 basis points, and it would rise by 6.42 percent if yield to maturity fell by 100 basis points. Figure 6.1 shows the change in price predicted by modified duration for given changes in yield to maturity (the solid line) compared with the change in price that would actually occur (the dashed line).

Convexity

In Figure 6.1, the line that represents the actual price response to a given change in yield to maturity is convex. The larger the increase in yield to maturity, the greater the magnitude of the error by which modified duration will overestimate the bond's price decline; the larger the decrease in yield to maturity, the greater the magnitude of the error by which modified duration will underestimate the bond's price rise.

This phenomenon is called convexity, and it arises for the following reason. As yield to maturity changes, a bond's duration changes as well. Modified duration is thus an accurate predictor of price change only for vanishingly small changes in yield to maturity. If yield to maturity is 10 percent, for example, modified duration

**Figure 6.1   Pricing Error of Modified Duration
(10-Year Bond with $100 Annual Coupon,
$1,000 Principal, and 10% Initial Yield to Maturity)**

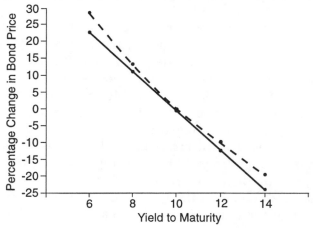

equals 6.14, which implies that a 100-basis-point change in yield to maturity will result in a 6.14 percent change in bond price. However, as yield to maturity increases to 10.25 percent, modified duration falls to 6.02, which implies smaller price changes for subsequent changes in yield to maturity.

The price response of a bond to changes in yield to maturity is consequently a function not only of the bond's modified duration but of its convexity as well. Whereas modified duration measures the sensitivity of bond prices to changes in yield to maturity, convexity measures the sensitivity of duration to changes in yield to maturity.

Convexity is more pronounced the farther apart the cash flows are. Imagine a bond that has 10 annual cash flows. If yield to maturity increases, the present value of the 10th cash flow will decrease the most, the present value of the ninth cash flow will decrease by a smaller amount, the present value of the eighth cash flow will decrease by yet a smaller amount, and so on. Duration will decrease as the more distant cash flows are assigned less and less weight. To the extent the cash flows are not far apart from each other, however, duration will not decrease that much because the changes in the weights associated with successive cash flows will be similar to each other.

Now consider a bond that has only two cash flows, one after the first year and one after the 20th year. If yield to maturity increases, the present value of the first cash flow will change by a significantly smaller amount than the change in the present value of the second cash flow. The weight assigned to the time to receipt of the first cash flow will thus decline only slightly, whereas the weight assigned to the time to receipt of the second cash flow will decline meaningfully, resulting in a more substantial change in the bond's duration.

Applications of Duration and Convexity

Duration and convexity are essential tools for fixed income portfolio management. Duration enables portfolio managers to act upon their convictions about interest rate shifts. If a manager expects interest rates to fall, she should increase the duration of her portfolio in order to leverage the price appreciation that will occur if she is correct. If she expects an increase in rates, she should of course reduce duration to protect her portfolio from price losses.

Duration and convexity are also useful for hedging a stream of liabilities. A portfolio manager can hedge a liability stream by constructing a portfolio of equal duration and convexity, as long as its present value equals the present value of the liabilities at the outset. If the present value of the liabilities exceeds the present value of the assets available for hedging, the duration of the portfolio must exceed the duration of the liabilities. The converse is true if the value of the portfolio exceeds the value of the liabilities. Moreover, modified duration relates the percentage change in price to absolute changes in yield to maturity. In order to hedge a portfolio of liabilities with a different value, duration must be adjusted to relate the dollar change in price to changes in yield to maturity.

Finally, a portfolio can be immunized from interest rate shifts by setting its duration equal to the investor's holding period. If interest rates rise, the capital loss will be offset by the gain from reinvesting the cash flows at higher yields. Conversely, if interest rates fall, the reduction in income resulting from reinvestment of cash flows at lower rates is offset by the capital gain. Of course, capital gains and losses are balanced by reinvestment gains and losses only to the extent that short-term rates and long-term rates move together. If long-term rates increase but short-term rates remain unchanged, the portfolio's income will not increase sufficiently to offset the capital loss; in this case, immunization will fail.

Conclusion

This chapter is intended to provide some elementary insights into the notions of duration and convexity. As such, I have ignored many of the complexities associated with these notions. For example, I have implicitly assumed throughout that a bond's cash flows are perfectly predictable. In fact, many bonds have call or put provisions that introduce an element of uncertainty to the cash flows. Moreover, the cash flows of mortgage-backed securities are uncertain because mortgage borrowers usually have the right to prepay their loans. These complexities can have a significant impact on the measurement of duration and convexity and their application to risk control. Those who are interested in interest rate risk should consult more advanced sources.[4]

Notes

1. F. Macaulay, *Some Theoretical Problems Suggested by the Movements of Interest Rates, Bond Yields and Stock Prices in the United States Since 1865* (New York: National Bureau of Economic Research, 1938).

2. For example, see M. Leibowitz, "How Financial Theory Evolves in the Real World—Or Not: The Case of Duration and Immunization," *The Financial Review*, November 1983.

3. This formula assumes that coupons are paid annually. If coupon payments occur more frequently, the yield to maturity should be divided by the number of discounting periods per year.

4. For a more thorough review of these issues, see F. Fabozzi and I. Pollack, eds., *The Handbook of Fixed Income Securities* (Homewood, IL: Dow Jones-Irwin, 1987), and R. Platt, ed., *Controlling Interest Rate Risk: New Techniques and Applications for Money Management* (New York: John Wiley & Sons, 1986).

7
The Term Structure of Interest Rates

This chapter addresses the term structure of interest rates. I begin by reviewing the various ways in which the term structure is measured. Then I present the major hypotheses that purport to explain the relationship between interest rates and term to maturity. Finally, I discuss a simple technique for estimating the term structure.

What Is the Term Structure of Interest Rates?

The term structure of interest rates, sometimes referred to as the *yield curve*, isolates the differences in interest rates that correspond solely to differences in term to maturity. As a first approximation, we can measure the term structure by measuring the relationship between the yields to maturity on government debt instruments and their terms to maturity. By focusing on government debt instruments, we control for differences in yield that might arise from credit risk.

The *yield to maturity* of a bond equals the internal rate of return that discounts its cash flows, including the coupon payments and the repayment of principal, back to the bond's current price. This relationship is described by equation (1):

$$P = \frac{C_1}{(1+y)} + \frac{C_2}{(1+y)^2} + \ldots + \frac{C_n}{(1+y)^n} + \frac{F}{(1+y)^n} \qquad (1)$$

where

P = current price,
C_1, C_2, C_n = coupon payments in periods 1 through n,
F = face value,
y = yield to maturity and
n = number of discounting periods.

The yield to maturity does not provide a particularly satisfying yardstick for measuring the term structure of interest rates, for two reasons. First of all, it is an unrealistic measure of a bond's yield because it assumes that all of a bond's cash flows are reinvested at the same rate. This assumption implies that a one-year instrument nine years hence will have the same yield as a 10-year bond today. Obviously, there is no reason to expect interest rates to evolve according to this assumption.

Second, because capital gains receive favorable tax treatment relative to income, bonds with the same term to maturity might have yields to maturity that differ according to the fraction of their return that arises from income versus price change.

To control for the differential tax treatment of coupons and price change, we can measure the term structure of interest rates from the yields on pure discount bonds. These bonds do not pay coupons. Instead, they are initially offered at a discount to their face value, so that their yield is equal to the annualized return resulting from their conversion to face value. The yield on a pure discount bond is referred to as the *spot rate of interest*.

We can think of a bond with predictable cash flows as a portfolio of pure discount bonds. In order to price coupon-bearing bonds using spot interest rates, we assign the yield of a pure discount instrument maturing in six months to the coupon payment six months from now and the yield of a one-year, pure discount instrument to the coupon due one year from now, proceeding in this fashion until we assign yields to all the bond's cash flows. This relationship is shown in equation (2). For purposes of simplification, equation (2) assumes that coupon payments occur annually.

$$P = \frac{C_1}{(1 + r_1)} + \frac{C_2}{(1 + r_2)^2} + \ldots + \frac{C_n}{(1 + r_n)^n} + \frac{F}{(1 + r_n)^n} \qquad (2)$$

where

r_1, r_2, r_n = spot rates of interest of pure discount bonds maturing in periods 1 through n.

As long as there is a reasonable supply of pure discount bonds at all relevant maturities, the spot rates of interest should reflect accurately the term structure of interest rates. It might be the case, however, that at particular maturities there is an inadequate supply of pure discount bonds, including coupons that have been stripped from coupon-bearing bonds. In this case, the yields on these bonds might misrepresent the term structure of interest rates. I will address this problem in the final section of this chapter.

We can also describe the term structure of interest rates by measuring the relationship between forward rates and term to maturity. The *forward rate* is the interest rate that will apply to an instrument commencing at some future date. It can be derived from the spot rates of interest.

Suppose that the spot rate of interest on a one-year instrument is 6.00 percent and that the spot rate of interest on a two-year instrument is 7.50 percent. If we were to contract to purchase a one-year instrument one year from now, what rate of interest should we expect for this instrument? The forward rate on a one-year instrument one year hence is determined so that an investor is indifferent between purchasing a two-year instrument today and holding it to maturity or purchasing a one-year instrument today and entering into a forward contract to purchase a one-year instrument one year from now. This equality is shown in equation (3).

$$(1 + r_2)^2 = (1 + r_1) \cdot (1 + f_{1,1}) \tag{3}$$

where
r_2 = spot rate for two-year instrument,
r_1 = spot rate for one-year instrument and
$f_{1,1}$ = one-year forward rate for one-year instrument.

If we substitute the one and two-year spot rates into equation (3), we find that the rate on a one-year instrument one year forward equals 9.02 percent.

Suppose that the market offers a one-year forward rate on a one-year instrument equal to 8.00 percent. In this case, we would invest in the two-year instrument today because we would be sure to earn a cumulative return of 15.56 percent ($1.075 \cdot 1.075 - 1$), compared with a cumulative return of 14.48 percent ($1.06 \cdot 1.08 - 1$) were we to invest in a one-year instrument today and a forward contract to invest in a one-year instrument one year hence. By the same logic, we would choose the one-year instrument and the forward contract if the forward rate were greater than 9.02 percent. The forward rate is governed by the law of one price, which states that equivalent cash flows must sell for the same price.

In general, we can derive the forward rate for any future date and for instruments of any maturity using equation (4), provided we can observe instruments with the requisite maturities today.

$$f_{t,n-t} = [(1 + r_n)^n/(1 + r_t)^t]^{1/(n-t)} \qquad (4)$$

where

$f_{t,n-t}$ = t-year forward rate for (n − t)-year instrument,
r_n = spot rate for n-year instrument and
r_t = spot rate for t-year instrument.

Yet another way in which we can represent the term structure of interest rates is to relate discount factors to maturity. The discount factor is equal to the reciprocal of one plus the spot rate raised to the maturity of the instrument, as shown in equation (5).

$$d(n) = 1/(1 + r_n)^n \qquad (5)$$

where

$d(n)$ = discount factor for n periods,
r_n = spot rate of interest for maturity n and
n = maturity of pure discount instrument.

The discount factor must fall between 0 and 1. It approaches 0 as the term to maturity approaches infinity, and it approaches 1 as the term to maturity approaches 0. Consider, for example, a situation in which the spot rates of interest are 8 percent across all maturities. Table 7.1 shows the discount factors corresponding to various maturities.

It is apparent from Table 7.1 that the discount factor is a nonlinear function of term to maturity. An increase of five years beginning with a term to maturity of one year reduces the discount factor by nearly 0.3 unit, whereas an increase of five years beginning in year 10 reduces it by less than 0.15 unit and beginning in year 15 by only 0.1 unit. As a percentage of value, however, the discount factor adjusts price proportionately with time. In all cases, an increase in term to maturity of five years reduces the value of the bond by 31.9 percent, given an 8 percent spot rate of interest.

What Determines the Term Structure of Interest Rates?

There are three hypotheses that are commonly cited to explain the term structure of interest rates—the expectations hypothesis; the liquidity premium hypothesis; and the segmented market hypothesis, also known as the preferred habitat hypothesis.

Table 7.1 Discount Factors When Spot Rate of Interest = 8%

Term to Maturity	Discount Factor
1	.9259
2	.8573
3	.7938
4	.7350
5	.6806
6	.6302
7	.5835
8	.5403
9	.5002
10	.4632
15	.3152
20	.2145

The *expectations hypothesis* holds that the current term structure of interest rates is determined by the consensus forecast of future interest rates. Suppose that the spot interest rate for a one-year instrument is 6 percent and that the spot rate of interest for a two-year instrument is 7 percent. According to the expectations hypothesis, this term structure arises from the fact that investors believe that a one-year instrument one year in the future will yield 8.01 percent, because an investor could achieve the same return by investing in a one-year instrument today and a one-year instrument one year from now as she could achieve by investing in a two-year instrument today. If the investor believes that the one-year rate one year in the future will exceed 8.01 percent, she will prefer to roll over consecutive one-year instruments as opposed to investing in a two-year instrument today. But if she anticipates that the one-year rate one year ahead will be less than 8.01 percent, she will opt for the two-year instrument today.

According to the expectations hypothesis, an upward sloping yield curve indicates that investors expect interest rates to rise. A flat yield curve implies that investors expect rates to remain the same. A downward sloping yield curve indicates that investors expect rates to fall.

It is important to distinguish the future spot rates that are implied by the current term structure from the forward rates on contracts available today. Although both rates are calculated in the same way and are therefore equal to each other, the interest rate on a forward contract must obtain in an arbitrage-free world, whereas the implied future spot rate is only a forecast, and not a particularly good one at that.

Based on the term structure in the previous example, the interest rate on a forward contract to purchase a one-year instrument one year from now must equal 8.01 percent. If the rate were lower, we could sell the forward contract together with a one-year instrument and use the proceeds to purchase a two-year instrument, thereby earning a riskless profit. If the rate on the forward contract were higher, we could reverse these transactions for a riskless profit.

It is not the case, however, that we would necessarily profit by combining purchases and sales today with purchases or sales in the future. Whether or not we profit would depend on the future, not forward, term structure of interest rates.

The distinction between actual forward rates and implied future rates is analogous to the difference between covered interest rate parity and uncovered interest rate parity. Covered interest rate parity is an arbitrage condition that explains the relationship between the spot exchange rate on a currency and its forward exchange rate. The forward rate is set such that an arbitrager cannot profit by borrowing in a low-interest-rate country, converting to the currency of a high-interest-rate country, lending at the higher interest rate and selling a forward contract to hedge away the currency risk. The cost of the hedge will precisely offset the interest rate advantage.

Uncovered interest rate parity posits that, on average, we cannot profit by borrowing in a low-interest-rate country, converting to the currency of a high-interest-rate country, and lending in that country without hedging away the currency risk. In effect, uncovered interest rate parity is nothing more than a statement that the forward rate is an unbiased estimate of the future spot rate. "Unbiased" does not mean that the forward rate is an accurate forecast of the future spot rate. It merely suggests that it does not systematically over- or under-estimate the future spot rate.

It is implausible that the expectations hypothesis fully accounts for the term structure of interest rates. As mentioned earlier, when the term structure of interest rates slopes upward, according to the ex-pectations hypothesis, investors expect interest rates to rise. Historically, the term structure has had an upward slope about 80 percent of the time. It seems unlikely that investors have expected interest rates to rise with that degree of frequency.

The expectations hypothesis is implausible for another reason. In order for it to be true, investors must believe that all bonds will generate the riskless return. Suppose that the spot rates of interest on a one-year instrument, a four-year instrument and a five-year instrument equal 6 percent, 7.5 percent and 8 percent, respectively. The expectations hypothesis implies that a four-year instrument one year in the future will have a rate of 8.51 percent. Based on today's term structure, we could purchase a pure discount bond with a face value of $1,000 maturing in five years for $680.58. If the implied future rate of 8.51 percent on a four-year discount bond is realized one year from now, we could then sell our four-year bond for $721.42, thereby earning a return of precisely 6.0 percent, which equals the riskless return on a one-year instrument.

Table 7.2 shows the implied term structure one year from now, given the present term structure along with the total return one would achieve during the ensuing year by purchasing discount bonds of various maturities should the implied future term structure materialize.

The implicit forecast that all bonds will yield the riskless return challenges credulity. It suggests that investors are indifferent to risk. Historically, the returns of long-term bonds have been higher on average and significantly more volatile than the returns on short-term instruments. This evidence suggests that investors demand and receive a premium in exchange for the higher volatility of long-term bonds.

Table 7.2 Total Return Implied by Forward Rates

Term to Maturity	Current Spot Rates	Implied Future Rates One Year Forward	Implied Total Return
1 Year	6.00%	7.00%	6.00%
2 Years	6.50%	7.50%	6.00%
3 Years	7.00%	8.00%	6.00%
4 Years	7.50%	8.51%	6.00%
5 Years	8.00%		6.00%

The higher historical returns of long-term bonds relative to shorter-term instruments lend credence to an alternative explanation of the term structure—the *liquidity premium hypothesis*. This hypothesis holds that investors are not indifferent to risk. They recognize that a bond's price is more sensitive to changes in interest rates, the longer its maturity, and they demand compensation for bearing this interest rate risk. Thus bonds with longer maturities typically offer a premium in their yields relative to shorter-term instruments in order to induce investors to take on additional risk. The extent of the premium increases with term to maturity but at a decreasing rate, for two reasons. Duration, a measure of a bond's price sensitivity to interest rate changes, increases at a decreasing rate with term to maturity.[1] Moreover, long-term interest rates are typically less volatile than short-term interest rates.

The notion that yields on longer-term instruments reflect a liquidity premium is consistent with the observation that the yield curve usually has an upward slope. Even when investors anticipate that interest rates will remain the same or decline slightly, a liquidity premium could still cause long-term rates to exceed short-term rates.

A third explanation of the term structure of interest rates is the segmented market hypothesis, which holds that groups of investors regularly prefer bonds within particular maturity ranges in order to hedge their liabilities or to comply with regulatory requirements. Life insurance companies, for example, have historically preferred to purchase long-term bonds, whereas commercial banks have favored shorter-term instruments. To the extent the demand of one group of investors increases relative to the demand of the other group, yields within the maturity range where relative demand has risen will fall relative to the yields within the maturity range where there is slack in demand.

Term Structure Estimation

If we were to trace a line through the yields on pure discount government bonds as they relate to maturity, it is unlikely that this line would form a smooth curve. Some of the observations would likely rise abruptly and some would likely fall abruptly. These apparent jumps might reflect the fact that some of the instruments have not traded recently; thus the observations are not contemporaneous with each other. Moreover, it may be the case that we have no observations for some maturities. In an effort to overcome these limitations, financial analysts have developed methods for estimating a smooth curve to represent the term structure.

One such method is called *spline smoothing*. This approach assumes that the discount factors corresponding to the spot interest rates are a cubic function of time to maturity, as shown in equation (6):

$$d(n) = a + b \cdot n + c \cdot n^2 + d \cdot n^3 \tag{6}$$

where
 $d(n)$ = discount factor for maturity n and
 n = term to maturity.

We estimate the coefficients of equation (6) by regressing the observed discount factors on three independent variables—term to maturity, its value squared and its value cubed. We then convert the estimated discount factor to its corresponding yield.

Table 7.3 shows a hypothetical observed term structure along with an estimated term structure based on the cubic spline method. The fitted regression equation from the observed term structure is as follows:

Discount Factor $= 1.01508 - 0.06206 \cdot n - 0.00017 \cdot n^2 + 0.000087 \cdot n^3$

Table 7.3 Cubic Spline Estimated Term Structure

Maturity	Observed Spot Rate	Observed Discount Factor	Estimated Discount Factor	Estimated Spot Rate
1	5.03%	.9521	.9529	4.94%
2	5.89%	.8918	.8909	5.94%
3	6.47%	.8285	.8297	6.42%
4	6.57%	.7753	.7696	6.77%
5	7.20%	.7064	.7112	7.05%
6	7.35%	.6534	.6552	7.30%
7	7.55%	.6008	.6019	7.52%
8	7.60%	.5565	.5519	7.71%
9	7.89%	.5049	.5057	7.87%
10	8.00%	.4632	.4639	7.98%

These estimated yields allow us to price bonds for which we do not have reliable observations. Furthermore, we may believe that the values along the smoothed curve represent yields toward which the observed yields will converge, thereby suggesting trading opportunities.

I have attempted to provide a broad overview of the term structure of interest rates. This topic is one of the most widely researched areas of finance; the interested reader will have no trouble pursuing more detailed analyses.[2]

Notes

1. For a discussion of duration, see Chapter 6.

2. For example, see S. Brown and P. Dybvig, "The Empirical Implications of the Cox, Ingersoll, Ross Theory of the Term Structure of Interest Rates," *Journal of Finance*, July 1986; J. Cox, J. Ingersoll and S. Ross, "A Reexamination of Traditional Hypotheses About the Term Structure of Interest Rates," *Journal of Finance*, September 1981; H. G. Fong and O. Vasicek, "Term Structure Modeling," *Journal of Finance*, July 1982; and C. Nelson and A. Siegel, "Parsimonious Modeling of Yield Curves," *Journal of Business* 60 (1987), no. 4.

8
Serial Dependence

The first thing one should know about serial dependence is that it has nothing to do with an addiction to Rice Krispies, cornflakes or oatmeal. *Serial dependence* refers to the notion that returns evolve nonrandomly; that is, they are correlated with their prior values.

One variation of serial dependence is called *mean reversion*. With mean reversion, returns revert to an average value or asset prices revert to an equilibrium value. If an asset is priced above its equilibrium value, its price will not change randomly; it will be more inclined to decrease than to increase. Conversely, if an asset is priced below its equilibrium value, it will be more likely to increase than to depreciate further.

Another variation of serial dependence is known as *trending*. In a trending pattern, a positive return is more likely to be followed by another positive return than a reversal, and a negative return is more likely to be succeeded by another negative return than a positive return.

Of course, some returns may conform to nonrandom patterns that are more complex than simple mean reversion or trending. For example, the returns in a series may be correlated not with their immediately prior returns, but with more distant prior returns. Alternatively, returns may be linearly independent of prior values but display serial dependence after some transformation.

The extent to which asset returns evolve nonrandomly has important consequences for financial analysis. First of all, if asset returns are nonrandom, then their variance will depend on the interval used to measure them. Instead of varying proportionately with the time interval, the variance of returns will vary at a varying rate. I will discuss some of the implications of this nonlinearity later.

Second, if investment returns are serially dependent, they are at least partly predictable. This result is of obvious interest because it raises the possibility that we can devise trading rules to generate abnormal profits.

How to Detect Serial Dependence

There are several ways to detect serial dependence. One of the simplest and most intuitive is to perform a *runs test*. In order to perform a runs test, we first compute the average value of the series. Then we designate every value that is above the mean as positive and every value that is below the mean as negative. Next we compute the number of runs in the series.

A run is an uninterrupted sequence of positive or negative values. For example, a sequence of four positive values (++++) would constitute a single run, whereas a sequence of four alternating values (+-+-) would constitute four runs. The expected number of runs in a random sequence is given by the following formula:

$$E(R) = \frac{2(n1)(n2)}{n1 + n2} + 1 \qquad (1)$$

where
  n1 = number of positive observations and
  n2 = number of negative observations.

A random series of 60 positive observations and 40 negative observations should have 49 runs. Significantly more than 49 runs would indicate that the duration of the series' typical run is shorter than we should expect from a random series. We would conclude, therefore, that the series is characterized by mean reversion. Significantly fewer than 49 runs would indicate that the duration of the series' typical run is longer than we should expect from a random series; the series is characterized by trends.

In order to determine whether or not the actual number of runs differs significantly from the expected number of runs, we must compute the standard deviation of runs. This is given by equation (2):

$$S = \sqrt{\frac{2(n1)(n2)[2(n1)(n2) - n1 - n2]}{(n1 + n2)^2 (n1 + n2 - 1)}} \qquad (2)$$

Once we know the standard deviation of the runs, we can compute a normal deviate by dividing the difference between the observed number of runs and the expected number of runs by the standard deviation. Based on 60 positive values and 40 negative values, the standard deviation of runs equals 4.77. If we observe only 39 runs, we should be about 96 percent confident that the series is nonrandom; because there are fewer runs than we would expect from a random sequence, we would conclude that the series trends. If we observe 59 runs, we would be equally confident that the series is nonrandom, but this time we would conclude that the series is mean reverting.

A runs test is limited because it deals only with direction. It depends only on whether an observation is above or below average and not on the extent to which the observation differs from the average. Statistical procedures that deal only with rank are referred to as *nonparametric procedures*.

We can also measure serial dependence with procedures that rely on the magnitude of the observations instead of just their rank. One obvious procedure is to test for *autocorrelation* by regressing the returns in a series on their prior values. If we regress a series on the immediately prior values, we test for first-degree autocorrelation. If we regress a series on the values preceding the immediately prior values, we test for second-degree autocorrelation.

A significantly positive correlation coefficient suggests that a series is prone to trends. A significantly negative correlation coefficient suggests that a series is characterized by mean reversion.

Another parametric procedure for measuring serial dependence is called a *variance ratio test.* If a sequence of returns is random and we compute several estimates of the variance based on different return intervals, the estimates should be linearly related to one another. Specifically, the variance estimated from two-day returns should be twice as large as the variance estimated from daily returns, and the variance estimated from quarterly returns should be three times as large as the variance estimated from monthly returns. If you prefer to think in terms of standard deviations, the standard deviation of quarterly returns should exceed the standard deviation of monthly returns by a factor equal to the square root of three.

The variance ratio is computed by dividing the variance of returns estimated from the longer interval by the variance of returns estimated from the shorter interval and then normalizing this value to one by dividing it by the ratio of the longer interval to the shorter interval:

$$VR = \frac{Vl/Vs}{l/s} \qquad (3)$$

where

Vl = variance estimated from longer interval returns,
Vs = variance estimated from shorter interval returns,
  l = number of periods in longer interval and
  s = number of periods in shorter interval.

Suppose, for example, we estimate the variance of annual returns as 4.0 percent and the variance of monthly returns, using the same measurement period, as 0.4 percent. Based on these estimates, the variance ratio equals 0.8333 [(4.0%/0.4%)/12].

A variance ratio of less than one suggests that the shorter-interval returns tend toward mean reversion within the duration of the longer interval. By contrast, a variance ratio that exceeds one suggests that the shorter-interval returns are inclined to trend within the duration of the longer interval.

Consider an extreme and obviously unrealistic example. Suppose we observe, each year for many years, the pattern of returns given in Table 8.1. Just by inspection, it is apparent that the monthly returns trend within a quarter and that the quarterly returns mean revert within a year. This result is confirmed by the variance ratio test. The variance of the monthly returns equals 0.01 percent, and the variance of the quarterly returns equals 0.09 percent, which corresponds to a variance ratio of 3.00.

Table 8.1 Hypothetical Return Series

	Monthly	Quarterly	Annual
January	1.00%		
February	1.00		
March	1.00	3.03%	
April	−1.00		
May	−1.00		
June	−1.00	−2.97%	
July	1.00		
August	1.00		
September	1.00	3.03%	
October	−1.00		
November	−1.00		
December	−1.00	−2.97%	−0.06%

Because the annual return is the same every year, the variance of the annual returns equals 0.0 percent. The variance ratio of annual returns to quarterly returns or to monthly returns thus also equals 0, demonstrating that mean reversion produces a variance ratio that is less then one.

Of course, whether or not a series is significantly nonrandom depends on the magnitude of the variance ratio and the number of observations from which it is estimated. Equation (4) shows how to calculate the normal deviate of a variance ratio that is estimated from overlapping observations:[1]

$$z(q) = \sqrt{n}(VR - 1)[2(2q - 1)(q - 1)/3q]^{1/2} \quad (4)$$

where
    n = number of observations used to estimate variance in denominator,
    VR = variance ratio and
    q = number of periods in interval used to estimate variance in numerator.

The use of overlapping observations helps to preserve a sufficient number of observations for estimating the variance in the numerator as we extend the interval.

The variance in the numerator of the variance ratio in equation (4) is computed slightly differently from the normal method. Because the variance in the numerator is estimated from overlapping returns, it is computed by squaring the differences, not from the average return of the longer-interval returns but rather from a quantity equal to the average of the shorter-interval returns multiplied by the number of periods in the longer interval. For example, if monthly returns are used to estimate the variance in the denominator and quarterly returns are used to estimate the variance in the numerator, then the numerator's variance is estimated as the average of the squared differences from the average monthly return times three.

It is also important to note that equation (4) depends on the assumption that the nonrandomness is not caused by heteroscedasticity, which is to say it does not arise because the variance changes through time. If heteroscedasticity is present, additional adjustments are required to determine whether or not the series is serially dependent.[2]

Investment Implications

As noted, if returns are serially dependent, variances estimated from longer-interval returns may not be proportional to variances estimated from shorter-interval returns. If returns are positively serially correlated, (i.e., trending), then variance should grow at an increasing rate as the return interval increases. If returns are negatively serially correlated (i.e., mean reverting), then variance should grow at a declining rate as the return interval increases.

This result has important consequences for asset allocation. Suppose we choose an asset mix by maximizing expected utility, which we define as expected return minus risk aversion times variance. If variance is proportional to time, our investment horizon does not affect our choice of asset mix. But if variance increases at an increasing rate with time, we would choose a more conservative asset mix, the longer our horizon. The opposite would hold if variance increased at a decreasing rate with time. We would be inclined to select a more aggressive asset mix over a longer horizon than we would select for a shorter horizon.

Suppose, for example, that a particular asset mix has an expected annual return of 10 percent and a variance of 4 percent, estimated from annual returns. If, at the margin, we are willing to sacrifice two units of expected return to reduce variance by one unit (that is, our risk aversion equals 2), this asset mix is expected to yield 0.02 units of utility, given a one-year horizon $(0.10 - 2 \times 0.04)$.

Now suppose that the variance ratio of five-year returns to one-year returns equals 1.1. This variance ratio implies that the annualized variance estimated from five-year returns equals 4.4 percent. The same asset mix is expected to yield only 0.012 annualized units of utility, given a five-year horizon. We must choose a more conservative asset mix to generate the same level of expected utility that we expect from the asset mix given a one-year horizon.

If the variance ratio of five-year returns to one-year returns equals 0.9 percent, the annualized variance estimated from five-year returns would equal 3.6 percent; the same asset mix would yield 0.028 units of expected utility. We would thus have to lower the risk of the asset mix in order to generate the same level of expected utility in one year that we could achieve given a five-year horizon. Table 8.2 summarizes these results.

Table 8.2 Expected Utility as a Function of Horizon When Returns Are Nonrandom

Investment Horizon	Annualized Expected Return	Risk Aversion	Annualized Variance	Expected Utility
1 Year	10.0%	2	4.0%	2.0%
5 Years (VR = 1.1)	10.0	2	4.4	1.2
5 Years (VR = 0.9)	10.0	2	3.6	2.8

Now consider the implications of serial dependence on option pricing. The value of an option is conditioned on five factors—the price of the underlying asset, the strike price, the riskless rate of interest, the time remaining to expiration and the volatility of the underlying asset. If we hold constant all the other factors, the value of an option increases with the volatility of the underlying asset because uncertainty raises the likelihood that the option will end up in the money.

If the returns of the underlying asset are positively serially correlated within a quarter, then the variance of quarterly returns will exceed three times the variance of monthly returns. Therefore, if we estimate the volatility of the underlying asset from monthly or higher-frequency returns, and then extrapolate this estimate according to the Black-Scholes assumption that variance changes linearly with time, we will underestimate the value of the three-month option. If the returns of the underlying asset mean revert, and we extrapolate the variance in accordance with the assumptions of Black-Scholes, we will overestimate the value of the longer-dated option.

We can extrapolate the annualized variance estimated from shorter intervals simply by multiplying it by the appropriate variance ratio. Similarly, we can extrapolate an annualized standard deviation by multiplying it by the square root of the appropriate variance ratio. For example, suppose our estimate of standard deviation is based on daily returns and we wish to estimate the value of an option that expires in three months. If the variance ratio of three-month returns to daily returns equals 1.21, we simply multiply the annualized standard deviation of daily returns by 1.10, the square root of the variance ratio, in order to value the three-month option.

If we believe that the returns of the underlying asset are serially dependent but that the market prices the option according to the Black-Scholes assumption that variance changes linearly with time, we might be able to profit by trading options on the same underlying asset but with different expiration dates. If the asset's returns trend within the horizon of a long-dated option, the long-dated option will be undervalued, on balance, relative to a short-dated option. We should, therefore, purchase the long-dated option and sell the short-dated option. By contrast, if the asset's returns mean revert within the horizon of the long-dated option, it will be overvalued relative to the short-dated option. We should thus sell the long-dated option and purchase the short-dated option.

If returns are serially dependent, it follows that they are partly predictable. We might therefore be able to devise profitable trading strategies. We might be able to exploit mean reversion with a simple linear investment rule. If the allocations of the assets in our portfolio change according to changes in their relative returns, for example, we might decide to change an asset's allocation by less than the return-induced change, anticipating that the asset return will revert toward its average level.

Suppose we allocate 50 percent of our portfolio to a risky asset that we believe mean reverts and the balance to a riskless asset that returns 0.5 percent per month. With changes in the risky asset's return, we will change the asset's allocation by an amount equal to –5 times the percentage change that would occur in a simple buy-and-hold portfolio. Table 8.3 shows how $100 invested according to this linear investment rule grows over one year compared with a 50/50 buy-and-hold strategy, assuming the risky asset's returns revert back and forth between +6.0 percent and –4.0 percent.

The linear investment rule generates a 2.24 percent incremental return relative to the buy-and-hold strategy. Its standard deviation is also less—7.67 percent compared with 8.85 percent for the buy-and-hold strategy. Of course, it is highly improbable that any return series would follow such a precise mean-reverting pattern.

Evidence of Serial Dependence

The preceding discussion invites the obvious question: *Are* returns serially dependent? Table 8.4 shows the variance ratios and their

Table 8.3 A Linear Investment Rule to Exploit Mean Reversion

Risky Asset Return	Linear Investment Rule		Buy/Hold Strategy	
	Risky Percent	Portfolio Value	Risky Percent	Portfolio Value
—	50.00%	100.00	50.00%	100.00
6.0%	43.34	103.25	51.33	103.25
−4.0	48.95	101.75	50.19	101.38
6.0	42.29	105.00	51.52	104.69
−4.0	47.86	103.53	50.37	102.78
6.0	41.20	106.77	51.70	106.14
−4.0	46.73	105.32	50.56	104.21
6.0	40.09	108.56	51.89	107.62
−4.0	45.56	107.14	50.75	105.65
6.0	38.94	110.36	52.08	109.13
−4.0	44.36	108.98	50.93	107.11
6.0	37.77	112.18	52.26	110.65
−4.0	43.12	110.84	51.12	108.60

significance for stocks, bonds and several currencies. The variance in the denominator is estimated from monthly returns. The significance is the normal deviate estimated by using equation (4).

According to the variance ratios in Table 8.4, monthly stock returns mean revert, monthly bond returns are random, and monthly currency returns trend. Only the French franc is significantly nonrandom, based on this measurement period.

The results in Table 8.4 suggest that we should at least be mindful of how we estimate volatility. It might not always be prudent to assume that variances change linearly with time. These results also suggest that we might be able to profit from trading rules designed to exploit serial dependence, although they do not inspire a great deal of confidence that simple trading rules will generate consistent profits. These results, however, might encourage one to investigate more complex structures of serial dependence.

Table 8.4 Variance Ratios, July 1973-June 1991

	Interval Used to Estimate Variance in Numerator		
	One Year	**Two Years**	**Three Years**
S&P 500			
Variance Ratio	0.88	0.46	0.34
Significance	−0.48	−1.54	−1.51
Government Bonds			
Variance Ratio	1.02	1.11	1.05
Significance	0.10	0.31	0.12
British Pound			
Variance Ratio	1.24	1.38	1.43
Significance	0.98	1.07	0.99
Deutschemark			
Variance Ratio	1.22	1.46	1.58
Significance	0.92	1.31	1.31
French Franc			
Variance Ratio	1.41	1.76	2.04
Significance	1.69	2.14	2.38
Japanese Yen			
Variance Ratio	1.37	1.39	1.40
Significance	1.55	1.10	0.92

Notes

1. For a derivation of a normal deviate based on overlapping observations, see A. Lo and A. MacKinlay, "Stock Market Prices Do Not Follow Random Walks: Evidence from a Simple Specification Test," *Review of Financial Studies*, Spring 1988.

2. A procedure for correcting for heteroscedasticity is given by Lo and MacKinlay, ibid. Please be aware, however, that it contains a typographical error. The numerator of Equation 19 should include the term "nq" in front of the summation sign.

9
Time Diversification

Suppose you plan to purchase a new home in three months, at which time you will be required to pay $100,000 in cash. Assuming you have the necessary funds, would you be more inclined to invest these funds in a riskless asset such as a Treasury bill or in a risky asset such as an S&P 500 index fund?

Now consider a second question. Suppose you plan to purchase a new home *10 years* from now, and that you currently have $100,000 to apply toward the purchase of this home. How would you invest these funds, given the choice between a riskless investment and a risky investment?

The only difference between these two scenarios is the length of your investment horizon. In the first case, you have a three-month horizon; in the second case, your investment horizon equals 10 years. If you are a typical investor, you would probably select the riskless investment for the three-month horizon and the risky investment for the 10-year horizon.

You might rationalize your choice as follows. Even though you expect stocks to generate a higher return over the long term, by investing in Treasury bills you are certain to have the requisite funds to satisfy your down payment three months from now. If you were to invest in stocks, there is a significant chance you could lose part of your savings, with little opportunity to recoup this loss, and be unable to meet the down payment requirement. But over a 10-year investment horizon, favorable short-term stock returns are likely to offset poor short-term stock returns; it is thus more likely that stocks will realize a return close to their expected return.

The Argument for Time Diversification

The notion that above-average returns tend to offset below-average returns over long horizons is called *time diversification*. Specifically, if returns are independent from one year to the next, the standard deviation of annualized returns diminishes with time. The distribution of annualized returns consequently converges as the investment horizon increases.

Figure 9.1 shows a 95 percent confidence interval of annualized returns as a function of investment horizon, assuming that the expected return is 10 percent and the standard deviation of returns equals 15 percent. These confidence intervals are based on the assumption that the returns are lognormally distributed; thus the standard deviation measures the dispersion of the logarithms of one plus the returns. It is apparent from Figure 9.1 that the distribution of annualized returns converges as the investment horizons lengthens.

It might also be of interest to focus on the notion of time diversification from the perspective of *losing* money. We can determine the likelihood of a negative return by measuring the difference in standard deviation units between a 0 percent return and the expected return. Again, if we assume that the S&P's expected return equals 10 percent and its standard deviation equals 15 percent, the expected return is 0.64 standard deviation above a 0 percent return, given a one-year horizon. This value corresponds to a 26 percent probability that the S&P 500 will generate a negative return in any one year.

Given a 10-year horizon, however, the annualized expected return is 2.01 standard deviations above an annualized return of 0.0 percent. There is only a 2.2 percent chance that the S&P 500 will produce a

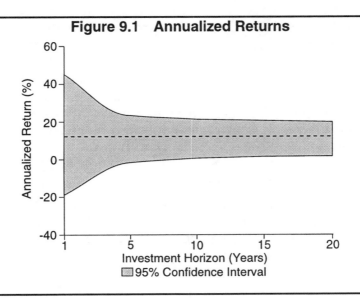

Figure 9.1   Annualized Returns

negative return, on average, over 10 years.[1] This does not imply that it is just as improbable to lose money in any *one* of these 10 years; it merely reflects the tendency of above-average returns to cancel out below-average returns.

Time Diversification Refuted

Several prominent financial economists, most notably Paul Samuelson, have argued that the notion of time diversification is specious for the following reason.[2] Although it is true that the annualized dispersion of returns converges toward the expected return with the passage of time, the dispersion of terminal wealth also diverges from the expected terminal wealth as the investment horizon expands.

This result implies that, although you are less likely to lose money over a long horizon than over a short horizon, the magnitude of your potential loss increases with the duration of your investment horizon. According to the critics of time diversification, if you elect the riskless alternative when you are faced with a three-month horizon, you should also elect the riskless investment when your horizon equals 10 years, or 20 years or, indeed, any duration.

This criticism applies to cross-sectional diversification as well as to temporal diversification. Suppose you have an opportunity to invest $10,000 in a risky venture, and you decline this opportunity because you think it is too risky. Would you be less averse to investing in 10 independent ventures, each of which has the same risk as the venture you declined and each of which requires a $10,000 investment?

You are clearly less likely to lose money by investing in 10 equally risky but independent ventures than by investing in just one of these ventures. The amount you could conceivably lose, however, is 10 times as great as your exposure in a single venture.

Now consider a third choice. Suppose you are offered a chance to invest a total of $10,000 in 10 independent but equally risky ventures. In this case you would invest only $1,000 in each of the 10 risky ventures. This investment opportunity diversifies your risk across the 10 ventures without increasing your total exposure. You might still choose not to invest, but your opposition to it should be less intense than it was to the first two alternatives.

Perhaps you are unpersuaded by these arguments. You reason as follows. Although it is true that the dispersion of terminal wealth increases with the passage of time or with the number of risky opportunities, the expected wealth of the risky venture also increases. The dispersion of wealth thus expands around a growing mean as the horizon lengthens or as the number of independent risky ventures increases.

Consider again the choice of investing in an S&P 500 index fund versus a riskless asset. Suppose the riskless asset has a certain 3 percent annual return compared with the S&P's 10 percent expected return and 15 percent standard deviation. Table 9.1 compares the dispersion of terminal wealth of the S&P 500 with the certain terminal wealth of the riskless investment.

After one year, the terminal wealth of an initial $100,000 investment in the S&P index fund ranges from $81,980 to $147,596 given a confidence interval of 95 percent, while the riskless investment grows with certainty to $103,000. After 10 years, the spread in the S&P investment's terminal wealth expands from $65,616 to $554,829, but it surrounds a higher expected wealth. Thus the lower boundary of the 95 percent confidence interval is greater than the initial investment. If the investment horizon is extended to 20 years, the lower boundary of the 95 percent confidence interval actually exceeds the terminal wealth of the riskless investment.

Although this line of reasoning might strike you as a credible challenge to the critics of time diversification, in the limit it fails to resurrect the validity of time diversification.[3] Even though it is true that the lower boundary of a 95 percent confidence interval of the S&P investment exceeds the terminal wealth of the riskless investment after 20 years, the lower boundary of a 99 percent confidence interval falls below the riskless investment, and the lower boundary of a 99.9

Table 9.1 Risky versus Riskless Terminal Wealth

	S&P 500 95% Confidence Interval		Riskless Asset Terminal Wealth
	Lower Boundary	Upper Boundary	
1 Year	$ 81,980	$147,596	$103,000
5 Years	83,456	310,792	115,927
10 Years	102,367	657,196	134,392
15 Years	133,776	1,304,376	155,797
20 Years	180,651	2,565,345	180,611

percent confidence interval is even worse. The growing improbability of a loss is offset by the increasing magnitude of potential losses.

It is an indisputable mathematical fact that if you prefer a riskless asset to a risky asset given a three-month horizon, you should also prefer a riskless asset to a risky asset given a 10-year horizon, assuming the following conditions are satisfied:

1. Your utility function is invariant to changes in your wealth.

2. You believe that risky returns are random.

3. Your future wealth depends only on investment results.

Risk aversion implies that the satisfaction you derive from increments to your wealth is not linearly related to increases in your wealth. Rather, your satisfaction increases at a decreasing rate as your wealth increases. You thus derive more satisfaction when your wealth grows from $100,000 to $150,000 than you do when it grows from $150,000 to $200,000. It also follows that a decrease in your wealth conveys more disutility than the utility that comes from an equal increase in your wealth.[4]

The financial literature commonly assumes that the typical investor has a utility function equal to the logarithm of wealth. Based on this assumption, I will demonstrate numerically why it is that your investment horizon is irrelevant to your choice of a riskless versus a risky asset.

Suppose you have $100.00. This $100.00 conveys 4.60517 units of utility [ln(100.00) = 4.60517]. Now consider an investment opportunity that has a 50 percent chance of a $\frac{1}{3}$ gain and a 50 percent chance of a $\frac{1}{4}$ loss. A $100.00 investment in this risky venture has an expected terminal wealth equal to $104.17, but it too conveys 4.60517 units of utility [50% × ln(133.33) + 50% × ln(75.00) = 4.60517]. Therefore, if your utility function is defined by the logarithm of wealth, you should be indifferent between holding onto your $100.00 or investing it in this risky venture. In this example, $100.00 is the certainty equivalent of the risky venture because it conveys the same utility as the riskless venture.

Now suppose you are offered an opportunity to invest in this risky venture over two periods, and the same odds prevail. Your initial $100.00 investment can either increase by $\frac{1}{3}$ with a 50 percent probability in each of the two periods or it can decrease by $\frac{1}{4}$ with a 50 percent probability in each of the two periods. Over two periods, the expected terminal wealth increases to $108.51, but the utility of the investment opportunity remains the same. You should thus remain indifferent between keeping your $100.00 and investing it over two independent periods.

The same mathematical truth prevails irrespective of the investment horizon. The expected utility of the risky venture will always equal 4.60517, implying that you derive no additional satisfaction by diversifying your risk across time. This result holds even though the standard deviation of returns increases approximately with the square root of time, while the expected terminal wealth increases almost linearly with time.

Table 9.2 shows the possible outcomes of this investment opportunity after one, two and three periods, along with the expected wealth and expected utility after each period. The possible wealth values are computed by linking all possible sequences of return. Expected wealth equals the probability-weighted sum of each possible outcome, while expected utility equals the probability-weighted sum of the logarithm of each possible wealth outcome.

This result does not require that you have a log wealth utility function. Suppose, instead, that your utility function is defined by minus the reciprocal of wealth. This utility function implies greater risk aversion than a log wealth utility function. You would thus prefer to hold onto your $100.00 given the opportunity to invest in a risky venture that has an equal chance of increasing by $1/3$ or decreasing by $1/4$. You would, however, be indifferent between a certain $100.00 and a risky venture that offers an equal chance of increasing by $1/3$ or decreasing by $1/5$.

Table 9.3 shows that the expected utility of this risky venture remains constant as a function of investment horizon, even though the expected terminal wealth grows at a faster pace than it does in the previous example. Again, time diversification would not induce you to favor the risky venture over a multiperiod horizon if you did not prefer it for a single-period horizon.

Time Diversification Resurrected

Now that you have been exposed to the incontrovertible truth that time does not diversify risk, would you truly invest the same in your youth as you would in your retirement? There are several valid rea-

Table 9.2 Utility = ln(Wealth)

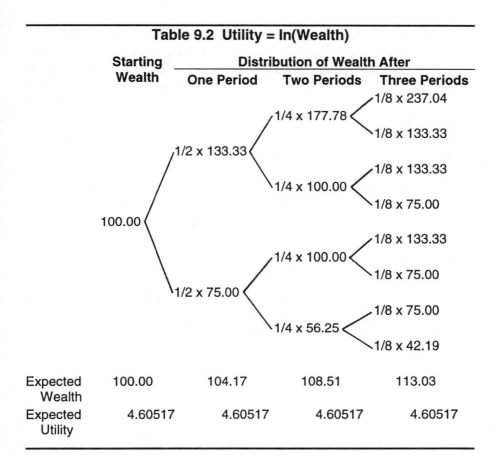

Starting Wealth	Distribution of Wealth After		
	One Period	Two Periods	Three Periods
Expected Wealth	100.00	104.17	108.51	113.03
Expected Utility	4.60517	4.60517	4.60517	4.60517

sons why you might still condition your risk posture on your investment horizon, even though you accept the mathematical truth about time diversification.

First, you may not believe that risky asset returns are random. Perhaps investment returns follow a mean-reverting pattern. If returns revert to their mean, then the dispersion of terminal wealth increases at a slower rate than implied by a lognormal distribution (the distribution that results from random returns). If you are more averse to risk than the degree of risk aversion implicit in a log wealth utility function, then a mean-reverting process will lead you to favor risky assets over a long horizon, even if you are indifferent between a riskless and a risky asset over a short horizon.[5]

Suppose, for example, that returns are not random. Instead, the risky venture in Table 9.3 has a 60 percent chance of reversing direction and, therefore, only a 40 percent chance of repeating its prior return. Table 9.4 reveals that expected utility rises from –0.010 over a single period to –0.00988 over two periods and to –0.00978 over three periods. Thus, if you believe in mean reversion and you are more risk averse than a log wealth investor, you should increase your exposure to risk as your investment horizon expands.

This result does not apply, however, to investors who have a log wealth utility function. These investors would not be induced to accept more risk over longer horizons, even if they believed in mean reversion.

Table 9.3 Utility = -1/Wealth

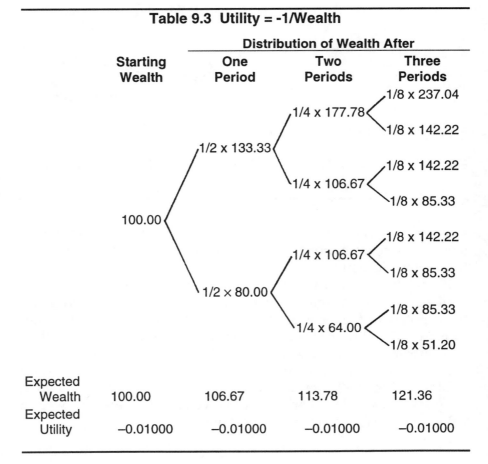

	Starting Wealth	One Period	Two Periods	Three Periods
Expected Wealth	100.00	106.67	113.78	121.36
Expected Utility	–0.01000	–0.01000	–0.01000	–0.01000

Table 9.4 Utility = -1/Wealth with Mean Reversion

	Distribution of Wealth After		
Starting Wealth	**One Period**	**Two Periods**	**Three Periods**

```
                                                          0.08 x 237.04
                                          0.20 x 177.78
                                                          0.12 x 142.22
                      1/2 x 133.33
                                                          0.18 x 142.22
                                          0.30 x 106.67
                                                          0.12 x 85.33
         100.00
                                                          0.12 x 142.22
                                          0.30 x 106.67
                                                          0.18 x 85.33
                      1/2 x 80.00
                                                          0.12 x 85.33
                                          0.20 x 64.00
                                                          0.08 x 51.20
```

	Starting Wealth	One Period	Two Periods	Three Periods
Expected Wealth	100.00	106.67	112.36	118.63
Expected Utility	−0.0100	−0.0100	−0.00988	−0.00978

Second, you might believe that the extremely bad outcomes required to justify the irrelevancy of time diversification would result from events or conditions that would have equally dire consequences for the so-called riskless asset, especially if you measure wealth in consumption units.

Third, even if you believe that returns are random, you might still choose to accept more risk over longer horizons than over shorter horizons because you have more discretion to adjust your consumption and work habits.[6] If a risky investment performs poorly at the beginning of a short horizon, there is not much you can do to compensate for this loss in wealth. If a risky investment performs poorly at the beginning of a long horizon, however, you can postpone consumption or work harder to achieve your financial goals. The argument against time diversification assumes implicitly that your terminal wealth depends only on investment performance.

Fourth, you may have a utility function that changes abruptly at a particular threshold. Consider, for example, a situation in which you require a minimum level of wealth to maintain a certain standard of living. Your lifestyle might change drastically if you penetrate this threshold, but further reductions in wealth are less meaningful. You might be more likely to penetrate the threshold given a risky investment over a short horizon than you would be if you invested in the same risky asset over the long run.

Moreover, even if you are not confronted with a real threshold, you might still behave as though you have a kinked utility function. Perhaps we can only process a finite set of possible outcomes, or maybe human nature leads us to ignore terrible outcomes that are extremely remote. Only the passage of time will reveal whether or not such behavior is prudent.

Finally, you are irrational. This does not mean you are a bad person. It simply implies that you behave inconsistently.

Notes

1. For a review of the relation between probability estimation and the dispersion of returns, see Chapter 2.

2. For example, see P. Samuelson, "Risk and Uncertainty: A Fallacy of Large Numbers," *Scientia*, April/May 1963; P. Samuelson, "Lifetime Portfolio Selection by Dynamic Stochastic Programming," *Review of Economics and Statistics*, August 1969; and Z. Bodie, A. Kane and A. Marcus, *Investments* (Homewood, IL: Irwin, 1989), 222–26.

3. I posed this argument in a letter to Paul Samuelson on December 2, 1991. In his reply, he eloquently and convincingly disabused me of the notion that a rising mean overcomes the increase in dispersion.

4. For a review of utility theory, see Chapter 3.

5. Samuelson addresses this result in P. Samuelson, "Longrun Risk Tolerance When Equity Returns Are Mean Reverting: Pseudoparadoxes and Vindication of 'Businessman's Risk,' "

in W. Brainard, W. Nordhaus and H. Watts, eds., *Macroeconomics, Finance and Economic Policy: Essays in Honor of James Tobin* (Cambridge, MA: MIT Press, 1991).

6. This idea is attributed to Zvi Bodie and William Samuelson, both of Boston University.

PART II

METHODOLOGY

10
Regressions

How can we predict uncertain outcomes? We could study the relations between the uncertain variable to be predicted and some known variable. Suppose, for example, that we had to predict the change in profits for the airline industry. We might expect to find a relation between GNP growth in the current period and airline profits in the subsequent period, because economic growth usually foreshadows business travel as well as personal travel. We can quantify this relation through a technique known as regression analysis.

Regression analysis can be traced to Sir Francis Galton (1822–1911), an English scientist and anthropologist who was interested in determining whether or not a son's height corresponded to his father's height. To answer this question, Galton measured a sample of fathers and computed their average height. He then measured their sons and computed their average height. He found that fathers of above-average height had sons whose heights were still above average but by a smaller amount. Galton termed this phenomenon "regression toward the mean."

Simple Linear Regression

To measure the relation between a single independent variable (GNP growth, in our earlier example) and a dependent variable (subsequent change in airline profits), we can begin by gathering some data on each variable—for example, actual GNP growth in each quarter of a given sample period and the change in the airline industry's profit over each subsequent quarter. We can then plot the intersects of these observations. The result is a scatter diagram such as the one shown in Figure 10.1.

The horizontal axis represents a quarter's GNP growth and the vertical axis represents the percentage change in profits for the airline industry in the subsequent quarter. The plotted points in the figure indicate the actual percentage change in airline profits associated with a given level of GNP growth. They suggest a positive rela-

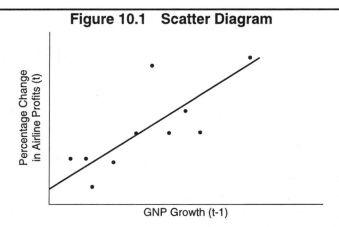

Figure 10.1   Scatter Diagram

tion; that is, as GNP increases so do airline profits. The straight line sloping upward from left to right measures this relation.

This straight line is called the *regression line*. It has been fitted to the data in such a way that the sum of the squared differences of the observed airline profits from the values along the line is minimized. The values along the regression line corresponding to the vertical axis represent the predicted change in airline profits given the corresponding prior quarter's GNP growth along the horizontal axis. The difference between a value predicted by the regression line and the actual change in airline profits is the error, or the residual.

Given a particular value for GNP growth, we can predict airline profits in the subsequent quarter by multiplying the GNP growth value by the slope of the regression line and adding to this value the intercept of the line with the vertical axis. The equation is:

$$\hat{Y}_1 = \hat{\alpha} + \hat{\beta} \cdot X_i$$

Here $\hat{Y}_1$ equals the predicted percentage change in airline profits, $\hat{\alpha}$ equals the intercept of the regression line with the vertical axis, $\hat{\beta}$ equals the slope of the regression line and X_i equals the prior quarter's growth in GNP.

We can write the equation for the *actual* percentage change in airline profits, given our observation of the prior quarter's GNP growth, by adding the error to the prediction equation:

$$Y_i = \hat{\alpha} + \hat{\beta} \cdot X_i + e_i$$

Here Y_i equals the actual percentage change in airline profits, and e_i equals the error associated with the predicted value.

Positive errors indicate that the regression equation underestimated the dependent variable (airline profits) for a particular value of the independent variable (GNP growth), while negative errors indicate that the regression equation overestimated the dependent variable. Figure 10.2 illustrates these notions.

Analysis of Variance

To determine whether or not the regression equation is a good predictor of the dependent variable, we can start by performing an analysis of variance. This involves dividing the variation in the dependent variable (change in airline profits) into two parts—that explained by variation in the independent variable (prior quarter's GNP growth) and that attributable to error.

In order to proceed, we must first calculate three values—the total sum of the squares, the sum of the squares due to regression and the sum of the squares due to error. The total sum of the squares is calculated as the sum of the squared differences between the observed values for the dependent variable and the average of those observations. The sum of the squares due to regression is calculated as the sum of the squared differences between the predicted values for the dependent variable and the average of the observed values for the dependent variable. Finally, the sum of the squares due to

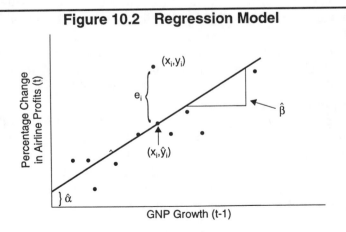

Figure 10.2   Regression Model

error is calculated as the sum of the squared differences between the observed values for the dependent variable and the predicted values for the dependent variable.

The ratio of the sum of the squares due to regression to the total sum of the squares equals the fraction of variation in the dependent variable that can be explained by variation in the independent variable. It is referred to as R-squared (R^2), or the coefficient of determination. It ranges in value from 0 to 1. A high value for R-squared indicates a strong relation between the dependent and independent variables, whereas a low value for R-squared indicates a weak relation.[1]

The square root of R-squared is called the correlation coefficient. It measures the strength of the association between the dependent and independent variables. In the case of an inverse relation—that is, where the slope of the regression line is negative—we must adjust the sign of the correlation coefficient to accord with the slope of the regression line. The correlation coefficient ranges in value from –1 to +1.

Residual Analysis

R-squared is only a first approximation of the validity of the relation between the dependent and independent variables. Its validity rests on several assumptions: (1) the independent variable (GNP growth in the example) must be measured without error; (2) the relation between the dependent and independent variables must be linear (as indicated by the regression line); (3) the errors, or residuals, must have constant variance (that is, they must not increase or decrease with the level of the independent variable); (4) the residuals must be independent of each other; and (5) the residuals must be normally distributed. Unless these assumptions are true, the measured relation between the dependent and independent variables, even if it has a high R-squared, may be spurious.

The importance of the first assumption is self-evident and should not require elaboration. The importance of some of the remaining assumptions may require some elaboration. In order to analyze the residuals, it is convenient to standardize each residual by dividing it by the standard error.[2] We can then plot the residuals to determine whether or not the above assumptions are satisfied.

Figure 10.3 shows a plot of standardized residuals. These seem to trace a convex curve. The errors associated with low values of the independent variable are positive; but they become increasingly negative with higher levels of the independent variable and then become positive again as the independent variable increases still more. In this case, it is apparent that the relation between the dependent and independent variables violates the assumption of linearity. The dependent variable increases with the independent variable but at a decreasing rate. That is to say, the independent variable has less and less effect on the dependent variable.

This pattern is characteristic of the relation between the level of advertising expenditures and sales, for example. Suppose a company distributes a product in several regions, and it varies the level of advertising expenditures across these regions to measure advertising's effect. The company will likely observe higher sales in a region where it advertises a little than in a region where it does not advertise at all. And as advertising increases from region to region, corresponding sales should also increase. At some level of sales, however, a region will start to become saturated with the product; additional advertising expenditures will have less and less impact on sales.

The obvious problem with using a linear model when the independent variable has a diminishing effect on the dependent variable is that it will overestimate the dependent variable at high levels of the independent variable. In many instances, we can correct this

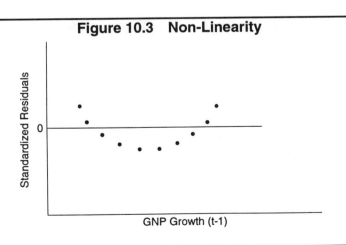

Figure 10.3   Non-Linearity

problem by transforming the values of the independent variable into their reciprocals and then performing a linear regression of the dependent variable on these reciprocals.

Figure 10.4 illustrates a case in which the absolute values of the standardized residuals *increase* as the values for the independent variable increase. In this case, the errors involved in predicting the dependent variable will grow larger and larger, the higher the value of the independent variable. Our predictions are subject to larger and larger errors. This problem is known as heteroscedasticity. It can often be ameliorated by transforming the independent variables into their logarithmic values.

Figure 10.5 shows a plot in which all the standardized residuals are positive with the exception of a single very large negative residual. This large negative residual is called an outlier, and it usually indicates a specious observation or an event that is not likely to recur. If we had included GNP growth in the last quarter of 1990 as one of the observations used to predict airline profitability, for example, we would have grossly overestimated airline profits in the first quarter of 1991; both business and personal air travel dropped precipitously in early 1991 because of the threat of terrorism stemming from the Gulf War. In this case, we would simply eliminate the outlying observation and rerun the regression with the remaining data.

In all these examples, the residuals form patterns rather than random distributions.

Figure 10.4   Heteroscedasticity

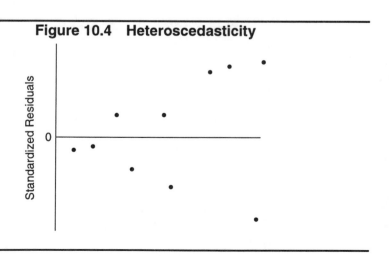

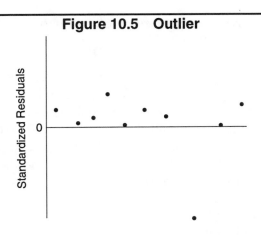

Figure 10.5   Outlier

In some cases the residuals might be correlated with one another, or autocorrelated. Without examining the residuals explicitly, we can test for first-order autocorrelation (correlation between successive residuals) by calculating a Durbin-Watson statistic. The Durbin-Watson statistic is approximately equal to $2(1 - R)$, where R equals the correlation coefficient measuring the association between successive residuals. As the Durbin-Watson statistic approaches 2, we should become more confident that the residuals are independent of each other (at least successively). Depending on the number of variables and number of observations, we can determine our level of confidence specifically.

With economic and financial data, it is often useful to transform the data into percentage changes, or first differences. This transformation often reduces autocorrelation.

Multiple Linear Regression

We have so far focused on simple linear regressions—that is, regressions between a dependent variable and a single independent variable. In many instances, variation in a dependent variable can be explained by variation in several independent variables. Returning to our example of airline profits, we may wish to include changes in energy prices as a second independent variable, given the relatively high operating leverage associated with the airline industry.

We can express this multiple regression equation as follows:

$$\hat{Y}_i = \hat{\alpha} + \hat{\beta}_1 \cdot X_{i1} + \hat{\beta}_2 \cdot X_{i2}$$

Here X_{i1} and X_{i2} equal the two independent variables (GNP growth and changes in energy prices) and $\hat{\beta}_1$ and $\hat{\beta}_2$ equal their coefficients.

It seems reasonable to expect that as fuel prices rise, profit margins in the airline industry will fall and vice versa. This would mean a negative relation between airline profits and energy prices. Thus $\hat{\beta}_2$ would be a negative value. But an increase in economic activity could increase demand for energy and contribute to a rise in energy prices. Thus the two independent variables, GNP growth and changes in energy prices, may not be independent of each other. This problem is known as multicolinearity.

Suppose we run two simple linear regressions using two independent variables. If the variables are independent of each other, then the sum of the R-squares from the two regressions will equal the R-squared from a multiple linear regression combining the two variables. To the extent that the independent variables are correlated with each other, however, the R-squared from the multiple regression will be less than the sum from the two simple regressions.

When the independent variables in a multiple regression are colinear, we must take care in interpreting their coefficients. The coefficients $\hat{\beta}_1$ and $\hat{\beta}_2$ in the above equation represent the marginal sensitivity of a change in airline profits to a one-unit change in GNP growth and to a one-unit change in energy prices in the prior quarter. If $\hat{\beta}_1$ equals 0.7 percent and $\hat{\beta}_2$ equals –0.15 percent, for example, we would expect airline profits to increase by 0.7 percent if GNP grew 1 percent in the prior quarter and energy prices remained constant. If energy prices increased by 1 percent in the prior quarter and GNP remained constant, we would expect airline profits to decrease by 0.15 percent. To the extent there is multicolinearity between the independent variables, these responses would not equal the sensitivity of airline profits to the same independent variables as measured by simple linear regressions.

Regression analysis is a powerful tool for the financial analyst. But, as I have attempted to demonstrate, the summary statistics from regression analysis can be misleading.

Notes

1. As part of their output, most regression packages include measures of statistical significance such as an F-value and a t-statistic. The F-value is computed as the ratio of the sum of the squares due to regression (adjusted by the degrees of freedom) to the sum of the squares due to error (also adjusted by the degrees of freedom). Its significance depends on the number of variables and observations. The t-statistic measures the significance of the coefficients of the independent variables. It is computed as the ratio of the coefficient to the standard error of the coefficient. The F-test and the t-test yield the same information for simple linear regressions, but not necessarily for multiple linear regressions.

2. The standard error measures the dispersion of the residuals around the regression line. It is calculated as the square root of the average squared differences of the observed values from the values predicted by the regression line. To estimate the average of the squared differences, we divide the sum of the squared differences by the number of observations less one.

11
Factor Methods

Financial analysts are concerned with factors, or common sources of risk that contribute to changes in security prices. By identifying such factors, analysts may be able to control a portfolio's risk more efficiently and perhaps even improve its return.

I will describe in general terms two approaches often used to identify factors. The first approach, called *factor analysis*, allows analysts to isolate factors by observing common variations in the returns of different securities. These factors are merely statistical constructs that represent some underlying source of risk; that source may or may not be observable. The second approach, called *cross-sectional regression analysis*, requires that we define a set of security attributes that measure exposure to an underlying factor and determine whether or not differences across security returns correspond to differences in these security attributes.

Factor Analysis

I begin with a nonfinancial, hopefully intuitive, example. I will apply the insights gained by this example to show how we might go about identifying the factors that underlie the stock market.

Suppose we wish to determine whether or not there are common sources of scholastic aptitude, based upon the grades of 100 students in the following nine courses—algebra, biology, calculus, chemistry, composition, French, geometry, literature and physics. We proceed as follows. First, we compute the correlation between the algebra grades of students one through 100 and their grades in each of the other eight courses. Then we compute the correlations between their biology grades and their grades in each of the seven other courses. We continue until we have computed the correlations between the grades of every pair of courses—36 correlations in all. Table 11.1 displays these hypothetical correlations.

Table 11.1 Correlations of Student Grades

	Bio.	Calc.	Chem.	Comp.	Fre.	Geo.	Lit.	Phy.
Algebra	.41	.93	.52	.31	.35	.88	.29	.59
Biology		.39	.94	.49	.44	.50	.31	.90
Calculus			.42	.29	.33	.95	.38	.60
Chemistry				.37	.41	.47	.40	.91
Composition					.87	.28	.94	.35
French						.32	.89	.46
Geometry							.38	.55
Literature								.43

That all these correlations are positive suggests the presence of a pervasive factor which is probably related to intelligence or study habits. In addition to this pervasive factor, there appear to be three other factors, or commonalities, in performance.

First, the variation in algebra grades is highly correlated with the variation in calculus and geometry grades. Moreover, performance in calculus is highly correlated with performance in geometry. The grades in these three courses, however, are not nearly as highly correlated with the grades in any of the other six courses. We might thus conclude that there is a common aptitude that underlies performance in these three courses.

Second, performance in biology is highly correlated with performance in chemistry and physics, and performance in chemistry is highly correlated with performance in physics. Again, performance in these courses does not correspond as closely with performance in any of the other courses. We might conclude that there is a common source of aptitude associated with biology, chemistry and physics.

Finally, the grades in composition, French and literature are all highly correlated with each other but not with the grades in any of the other courses. This leads us to deduce the presence of a third factor.

Our next task is to identify these factors. Here we must rely on our intuition. We might reasonably conclude that one of the common sources of scholastic aptitude is skill in mathematics or quantitative methods, because we observe high correlations between performances in the three math courses. Aptitude in science appears to be another common factor, given the high correlations in the three science courses. The remaining source of common variation in course grades pertains to composition, French and literature; we might label this factor verbal aptitude.

We do not actually observe the underlying factors. We merely observe that a student who performs well in algebra is more likely to perform well in geometry and calculus than in French. From this observation, we infer that there is a particular aptitude that helps to explain performance in algebra, calculus and geometry but not in French. This aptitude is the factor.

We should note that these results do not imply that performance in a given course is explained by a single factor. If such were the case, we would observe only correlations of 1 and 0. This point is underscored by the fact that the variation in physics grades is more highly correlated with performances in algebra, calculus and geometry than it is with performances in composition, French and literature. This result is intuitively pleasing, in that physics depends more on mathematics than do composition, French and literature. We might therefore conclude that performance in physics is primarily explained by aptitude in science, but that it is also somewhat dependent on math skills.

Now we will substitute stock performance for scholastic performance.

Factors in Stock Returns

Suppose we wish to determine the factors that underlie performance in the stock market. We begin by calculating the daily returns of a representative sample of stocks during some period. In this study, the stocks are analogous to courses, the days in the period are analogous to students, and the returns are analogous to grades.

To isolate the factors that underlie stock market performance, we begin by computing the correlations between the daily returns of each stock and the returns on every other stock. Then we seek out groups consisting of stocks that are highly correlated with each other but not with the stocks outside the group.

For example, we might observe that stock one's returns are highly correlated with the returns of stocks 12, 21, 39, 47, 55, 70 and 92, and that the returns of the other stocks in this group are all highly correlated with each other. From this observation, we might conclude that the returns of these stocks are explained at least in part by a common factor. We proceed to isolate other groups of stocks whose returns are highly correlated with each other, until we isolate all the groups that seem to respond to a common source of risk.

Our next task is to identify the underlying source of risk for each group. Suppose that a particular group consists of utility companies, financial companies and a few other companies that come from miscellaneous industries but that all have especially high debt-to-equity ratios. We might reasonably conclude that interest rate risk is a common source of variation in the returns of this group of stocks. Another group might be dominated by stocks whose earnings depend on the level of energy prices; we might thus hypothesize that the price of energy is another source of risk. Yet another group might include companies across many different industries that have in common the fact that they derive a large fraction of their earnings from foreign operations; we might conclude that exchange rate risk is yet another factor.

We must first rely on our intuition to identify the factor that underlies the common variation in returns among the member stocks. Then we can test our intuition as follows. We define a variable that serves as a proxy for the *unanticipated* change in the factor value. We regress the returns of stocks that seem to depend on our hypothesized factor with the unanticipated component of the factor value. It is important that we isolate the unanticipated component of the factor value, because stock prices should not respond to an anticipated change in a factor. It is new information that causes investors to reappraise the prospects of a company.

Suppose, for example, we identify inflation as a factor. If the Consumer Price Index is expected to rise 0.5 percent in a given month and it rises precisely by that amount, then the prices of inflation-sensitive stocks should not change in response. If the CPI rises 1.5 percent, however, then the prices of these stocks should change in response. In order to test whether or not a particular time series represents a factor, we must therefore model the unanticipated component of its changes.

A reasonable approach for modeling the unanticipated component of inflation is to regress inflation on its prior values under the assumption that the market's outlook is conditioned by past experience. The errors, or residuals, from this regression represent the unanticipated component of inflation. We thus regress these residuals on the returns of the stocks we believe to be dependent on an inflation factor to determine if inflation is indeed a factor.

The approach I have just described is heuristic. It is designed to expose factors by identifying groups of stocks with common price variations. Its intuitive appeal is offset by the fact that it produces factors that explain only part of the variation in returns. Moreover, these factors are not necessarily independent of each other.

With a more advanced mathematical technique—called *maximum likelihood factor analysis*—we can identify several linear combinations of securities, comprised of both long and short positions, that explain virtually all the covariation in the returns of a sample of securities.[1] These linear functions are called *eigenvectors*, and the sensitivity of a particular security to an eigenvector is called an *eigenvalue*.[2].

Instead of groups of highly correlated stocks, this approach yields precise linear combinations of stocks that represent independent sources of common variation in returns. In effect, the eigenvectors are the factors. Not only are the factors derived in this fashion independent of each other, but we can derive as many factors as necessary to explain as much of the covariation in a portfolio as we would like.

In order to label these factors, we proceed as described earlier. We determine whether or not the returns of these linear combinations of stocks correlate with the unanticipated changes in the variables that proxy for the factors. Within this context, we represent a security's return as follows:

$$R_i = \alpha_i + b_{i1} \cdot F_1 + b_{i2} \cdot F_2 + \ldots + b_{in} \cdot F_n + e_i$$

where

R_i = the return of security i,

α_i = a constant,

b_{i1} = the sensitivity of security i to factor 1,

b_{i2} = the sensitivity of security i to factor 2,

b_{in} = the sensitivity of security i to factor n,

F_1 = the first factor representing common variation
    in security returns,

F_2 = the second factor representing common variation
    in security returns,

F_n = the nth factor representing common variation
in security returns, and

e_i = variation in return that is specific to the ith security.

Issues of Interpretation

Factors derived through factor analysis, whether we employ the heuristic approach described earlier or the more formal approach, are not always amenable to interpretation. It may be that a particular factor cannot be proxied by a measurable economic or financial variable. Instead, the factor may reflect a combination of several influences, some perhaps offsetting, that came together in a particular way unique to the selected measurement period and the chosen sample of securities. In short, factors may not be definable. Moreover, factors derived through factor analysis may not persist through time, or factor 1 in one test may be factor 5 in another test.

We thus face the following tradeoff with factor analysis. Although we can account for nearly all a sample's common variation in return with independent factors, we may not be able to assign meaning to these factors, or even know if they represent the same sources of risk from period to period or sample to sample. Below we consider an alternative procedure called cross-sectional regression analysis.

Cross-Sectional Regression Analysis

Whereas factor analysis reveals covariation in returns and challenges us to identify the sources of this covariation, cross-sectional regression analysis requires us to specify the sources of return covariation and challenges us to affirm that these sources do indeed correspond to differences in return.

Here is how we proceed. Based upon our intuition and prior research, we hypothesize attributes that we believe correspond to differences in stock returns. For example, we might believe that highly leveraged companies perform differently from companies with low debt, or that performance varies according to industry affiliation. In either case, we are defining an attribute—not a factor. The factor that causes low-debt companies to perform differently from high-debt companies most likely has something to do with interest rates. Industry affiliation, of course, measures sensitivity to factors that affect industry performance, such as defense spending or competition.

Once we specify a set of attributes that we feel measure sensitivity to the common sources of risk, we perform the following regression. We regress the returns across a large sample of stocks during a given period—say a month—on the attribute values for each of the stocks as of the beginning of that month. Then we repeat this regression over many different periods. If the coefficients of the attribute values are not zero and are significant in a sufficiently high number of the regressions, we conclude that differences in return across the stocks relate to differences in their attribute values.

According to this approach, a security's return in a particular period equals:

$$R_i = \alpha + \lambda_1 \cdot b_{i1} + \lambda_2 \cdot b_{i2} + \ldots + \lambda_n \cdot b_{in} + e_i$$

where
   R_i = the return of security i,
   α = a constant,
   λ_1 = the marginal return to attribute 1,
   λ_2 = the marginal return to attribute 2,
   λ_n = the marginal return to attribute n,
   b_{i1} = attribute 1 of security i,
   b_{i2} = attribute 2 of security i,
   b_{in} = attribute n of security i, and
   e_i = the unexplained component of security i's return.

It is not necessary for the coefficients in the above formula to be significantly positive or negative on average over all the regressions. In some periods there may be positive returns associated with an attribute and in some periods there may be negative returns associated with an attribute; hence the average value for a coefficient over many regressions may be zero. Nonetheless, the attribute would still be important if the coefficient were not zero in a large number of the regressions.

We can measure the extent to which a coefficient is significant in a particular regression by its t statistic. The t statistic equals the value of the coefficient divided by its standard error. A t statistic of 1.96 implies that the likelihood of observing a significant coefficient by chance is only 5 percent. In order to be confident that a particular attribute helps to explain differences across security returns, we should observe a t statistic for its coefficient of 1.96 or greater in more than 5 percent of the regressions. Otherwise, it is possible that the attribute occasionally appears significant merely by chance.

Which Approach Is Better?

I have described two approaches for identifying common sources of variation in stock performance—factor analysis and cross-sectional regression analysis. There are pros and cons with both approaches. Through factor analysis, we can isolate independent sources of common variation in returns that explain nearly all of a portfolio's risk. It is not always possible, however, to attach meaning to these sources of risk. They may represent accidental and temporary confluences of myriad factors. Because we cannot precisely define these factors, it is difficult to know whether they are stable or simply an artifact of the chosen measurement period or sample.

As an alternative to factor analysis, we can define a set of security attributes we know are observable and readily measurable and, through cross-sectional regression analysis, test them to determine if they help explain differences in returns across securities. With this approach we know the identity of the attributes, but we are limited in the amount of return variation we are able to explain. Moreover, because the attributes are typically codependent, it is difficult to understand the true relationship between each attribute and the return. Which approach is more appropriate depends on the importance we attach to the identity of the factors versus the amount of return variation we hope to explain with independent factors.

Why Bother with Factors?

At this point you may question why we should bother to search for factors or attributes in the first place. Why not address risk by considering the entire covariance matrix, as originally prescribed by Markowitz?[3]

There are two reasons why we might prefer to address risk through a limited number of factors. A security's sensitivity to a common source of risk may be more stable than its sensitivity to the returns of all the other securities in the portfolio. If this is true, then we can control a portfolio's risk more reliably by managing its exposure to these common sources.

The second reason has to do with parsimony. If we can limit the number of sources of risk, we might find that it is easier to control risk and to improve return simply because we are faced with fewer parameters to estimate.

I have attempted to provide a flavor for the statistical methodology that underlies the search for common sources of return variation without prejudice toward one method or the other. The choice of a particular approach should depend on one's specific needs, one's biases, and a thorough understanding of the merits and limitations of each approach.

Notes

1. For a review of this methodology, see K. G. Joreskog, *Statistical Estimation in Factor Analysis* (Stockholm: Almqvist & Wiksell, 1963).

2. For a discussion of eigenvectors and eigenvalues, see A. C. Chiang, *Fundamental Methods of Mathematical Economics* (New York: McGraw-Hill, 1974), pp. 340-45.

3. For a review of Markowitz' approach for estimating portfolio risk, see Chapter 1.

12

Estimating Volatility: Part 1

Volatility is important to financial analysts for several reasons. Perhaps most obvious, estimates of volatility, together with information about central tendency, allow us to assess the likelihood of experiencing a particular outcome. For example, we may be interested in the likelihood of achieving a certain level of wealth by a particular date, depending on our choice of alternative investment strategies. In order to assess the likelihood of achieving such an objective, we must estimate the volatility of returns for each of the alternative investment strategies.

Financial analysts are often faced with the task of combining various risky assets to form efficient portfolios—portfolios that offer the highest expected return at a particular level of risk.[1] Again, it is necessary to estimate the volatility of the component assets. Also, the valuation of an option requires us to estimate the volatility of the underlying asset. These are but a few examples of how volatility estimates are used in financial analysis.

Historical Volatility

The most commonly used measure of volatility in financial analysis is standard deviation. Standard deviation is computed by measuring the difference between the value of each observation in a sample and the sample's mean, squaring each difference, taking the average of the squares and then determining the square root of this average.

Suppose, for example, that during a particular month we observe the daily returns shown in column 1 in Table 12.1. The average of the returns in column 1 equals 0.28 percent. Column 2 shows the difference between each observed return and this average return. Column 3 shows the squared values of these differences. The average of the squared differences—0.0167 percent—equals the variance of the returns. (In computing the variance, we divide by the number of observations less one, because we used up one degree of freedom to compute the average of the returns.) The square root of the vari-

Table 12.1 Standard Deviations of Return

Day	1 Return (%)	2 Return – Average (%)	3 Squared Difference (%)
1	1.00	0.72	0.0052
2	1.50	1.22	0.0149
3	2.10	1.82	0.0332
4	−0.40	−0.68	0.0046
5	1.00	0.72	0.0052
6	−1.40	−1.68	0.0281
7	0.45	0.17	0.0003
8	−0.75	−1.03	0.0106
9	1.00	0.72	0.0052
10	1.40	1.12	0.0126
11	−2.00	−2.28	0.0519
12	1.00	0.72	0.0052
13	−1.50	−1.78	0.0316
14	0.35	0.07	0.0001
15	−0.30	−0.58	0.0033
16	1.00	0.72	0.0052
17	0.00	−0.28	0.0008
18	−0.60	−0.88	0.0077
19	−1.20	−1.48	0.0218
20	2.90	2.62	0.0688
Average (%)	0.28		0.0167
Square Root (%)			1.2904

ance—1.2904 percent—equals the standard deviation of the daily returns.

In this example, the standard deviation measures the volatility of daily returns. It is typical in financial analysis to annualize the standard deviation. Unlike rates of return, which increase proportionately with time, standard deviations increase with the square root of time. We can take two approaches to converting a daily standard deviation into an annual standard deviation.

We can reconvert the standard deviation back into a variance by squaring it. Then we multiply the variance by 260 (the number of trading days in a year) and take the square root of this value to get the annualized standard deviation:

$$0.012904^2 = 0.000167$$

$$0.000167 \cdot 260 = 0.0433$$

$$\sqrt{0.0433} = 0.2081$$

Alternatively, we can multiply the daily standard deviation by the square root of 260 to determine the annualized value. This is algebraically equivalent to the first approach:

$$\sqrt{260} = 16.1245$$

$$0.012904 \cdot 16.1245 = 0.2081$$

The approach I have just described for estimating the standard deviation from historical returns yields an estimate that may lead to inexact inferences about the dispersion of returns. The inexactitude arises because the dispersion of investment returns conforms to a lognormal distribution, rather than a normal distribution, owing to the effect of compounding. We can attain more precise inferences by calculating the standard deviation of the logarithms of one plus the returns. Table 12.2 shows those calculations.

Comparing the standard deviation from Table 12.1 with the standard deviation from Table 12.2, we see that it does not make much difference which approach we use given this short measurement interval. As the measurement interval lengthens, however, the distinction becomes more important.

Implied Volatility

As we have seen, estimating volatility from historical data is fairly straightforward. Unfortunately, the result may not be the best estimate if volatility is unstable through time. In the fall of 1979, for example, the Federal Reserve changed its operating policy with respect to its management of the money supply and interest rates. Over the 10 years ending in 1978, the annualized standard deviation for long-term corporate bonds was a little less than 8 percent. In the subsequent 10-year period, from 1979 through 1988, the annualized standard deviation for long-term corporate bonds rose to more than

Table 12.2 Standard Deviations of Logarithmic Returns

Day	1 Log (1 + Return) (%)	2 Log – Average (%)	3 Squared Difference (%)
1	1.00	0.73	0.0053
2	1.49	1.22	0.0149
3	2.08	1.81	0.0327
4	−0.40	−0.67	0.0045
5	1.00	0.73	0.0053
6	−1.41	−1.68	0.0282
7	0.45	0.18	0.0003
8	−0.75	−1.02	0.0104
9	1.00	0.73	0.0053
10	1.39	1.12	0.0126
11	−2.02	−2.29	0.0524
12	1.00	0.73	0.0053
13	−1.51	−1.78	0.0317
14	0.35	0.08	0.0001
15	−0.30	−0.57	0.0032
16	1.00	0.73	0.0053
17	0.00	−0.27	0.0007
18	−0.60	−0.87	0.0076
19	−1.21	−1.48	0.0218
20	2.86	2.59	0.0671
Average (%)	0.27		0.0166
Square Root (%)			1.2867
Annualized Standard Deviation (%)			20.75

13 percent. Clearly, historical precedent made a poor guide for estimating bond market volatility in the 1980s.

As an alternative to historical data, we can infer the investment community's consensus outlook for the volatilities of many assets by examining the prices at which options on these assets trade. These implied volatilities presumably reflect all current information that impinges on an asset's volatility.

The value of an option depends on five factors—the current price of the underlying asset; the strike price, or price at which the option can be exercised; the time remaining until expiration; the riskless rate of interest; and the volatility of the underlying asset. We know the strike price and the time remaining until expiration from the terms of the option contract. The price of the underlying asset and the riskless rate of interest can be determined from a variety of market quote services. The only factor that we do not know with certainty is the volatility of the underlying asset. In order to determine volatility, we can substitute various values into the option pricing formula until the solution to this formula equals the price at which the option is trading.

Consider a call option with 90 days to expiration and a strike price of $295, written on an underlying asset currently priced at $300. Suppose the annualized riskless rate of interest is 8 percent and the option trades for $15. In order to determine the standard deviation, or implied volatility, consistent with the price of this option, we start by assuming some value for volatility and use this value in the following Black-Scholes option-pricing formula:

$$C = S \cdot N(D) - Xe^{-rT} \cdot N(D - \sigma\sqrt{T}) \tag{1}$$

where

   S = price of underlying asset,
   X = strike price,
   T = time remaining until expiration,
   r = instantaneous riskless rate of interest, $\ln(1 + r)$,[2]
   $D = (\ln(S/X) + (r + \sigma^2/2) \cdot T)(\sigma \cdot \sqrt{T})$
   $\ln(\ )$ = natural log,
   σ = standard deviation (volatility) of underlying asset returns
   $N(\ )$ = cumulative normal distribution function.[3]

Suppose we use the historical volatility over the previous 90 days—say, 20 percent. By substituting this value and the values we assigned earlier into equation (1), we find that D equals 0.401. Thus C, the option value, is calculated as:

$$C = 300 \cdot N(0.401) - 295e^{-0.077(90/365)} \cdot N(0.401 - 0.2 \cdot \sqrt{90/365})$$

$$C = 17.69$$

This estimated value is greater than the price at which the option currently trades. We must therefore lower our estimate for volatility.

Suppose we next try a value of 12 percent. Based on this volatility assumption, the option value equals $13.50; this is less than the actual price of $15, implying that we should raise our estimate.

If we continue substituting various volatility values into the Black-Scholes formula, we will eventually discover that a volatility estimate of 14.96 percent is consistent with an option value of $15—the price at which the option is currently trading. This 14.96 percent is the implied volatility, given the current values for the underlying asset, the option and the riskless rate and given the terms of the option contract.

Newton-Raphson Method

Of course, as we are solving for the implied volatility, the prices of the underlying asset and the option may be changing. We need a reasonably quick way to arrive at the implied volatility. The Newton-Raphson Method is one way.

According to the Newton-Raphson Method, we start with some reasonable estimate for volatility and evaluate the option using this estimate. Unless we are unusually lucky, however, we will not arrive at the correct value for implied volatility on our first try. We therefore revise our initial volatility estimate by subtracting an amount equal to the estimated option value minus the option's actual price, divided by the derivative of the option formula with respect to volatility evaluated at our estimate for volatility. This derivative is shown below:

$$\partial C / \partial \sigma = S \cdot \sqrt{T} \cdot (1/\sqrt{2\pi})e^{-D^2/2}$$

where
$\pi = 3.1416$ and
$e = 2.7183$.
C, S, T and D are as defined earlier.

Our earlier example used an assumed volatility of 20 percent. Using this assumption, the derivative for the Newton-Raphson Method is:

$$\partial C / \partial \sigma = 300 \cdot \sqrt{90/365} \cdot (1/\sqrt{2\pi})e^{-0.401^2/2},$$

$$\partial C / \partial \sigma = 54.64$$

The volatility of 20 percent resulted in an option value of $17.69. We compute the Newton-Raphson volatility estimate as follows:

$$\text{N–R Estimate} = 0.20 - (17.69 - 15)/54.64$$

$$= 0.1507$$

A volatility estimate of 15.07 percent results in an option value of $15.06. One more iteration yields a volatility estimate of 14.96 percent, for an option price of $15.

Method of Bisection

The efficiency of the Newton-Raphson Method depends to a certain extent on the choice of the initial volatility estimate. An alternative search procedure, which tends to be less sensitive to the initial volatility estimate, is called the Method of Bisection.[4] This approach is more intuitive. We start by choosing a low estimate for volatility corresponding to a low option value and a high estimate for volatility corresponding to a high option value.

For example, suppose we start with a low estimate of 10 percent and a high estimate of 30 percent. Given the assumptions from our previous example, the corresponding option values are $12.56 and $23.27. Our next estimate for volatility is found by interpolation, as shown below:

$$\text{New Estimate} = \sigma_L + (C - C_L) \cdot (\sigma_H - \sigma_L)/(C_H - C_L)$$

$$0.1456 = 0.1 + (15 - 12.56) \cdot (0.3 - 0.1)/(23.27 - 12.56)$$

$$0.1494 = 0.1456 + (15 - 14.79) \cdot (0.3 - 0.1456)/(23.27 - 14.79)$$

$$0.1496 = 0.1494 + (15 - 14.99) \cdot (0.3 - 0.1494)/(23.27 - 14.99)$$

If the option value corresponding to our interpolated estimate for volatility is below the actual option price, we replace our low volatility estimate with the interpolated estimate and repeat the calculation. If the estimated option value is above the actual option price, we replace the high volatility estimate with the interpolated estimate and proceed accordingly. When the option value corresponding to our volatility estimate equals the actual price of the option, we have arrived at the implied volatility for that option.

Historical versus Implied Volatility

Is it better to estimate volatility from historical observations or to infer it from the prices at which options trade? The answer, of course, depends on the quality of the inputs. If volatility is stationary through time, and we have reliable prices from which to estimate returns, then historical volatility is a reasonably good indicator of subsequent volatility. Unfortunately, and especially over short measurement intervals, nonrecurring events or conditions often cause volatility to shift up or down temporarily, so that historical volatility will over- or underestimate subsequent volatility. To the extent that the investment community recognizes the transitory nature of these nonrecurring events, implied volatility may provide a superior estimate of subsequent volatility. In estimating implied volatility, however, we must use contemporaneous observations for the inputs to the Black-Scholes formula.

The following procedure provides an intuitively appealing test of whether historical or implied volatility is a superior forecaster of actual volatility. First, estimate historical volatility in periods one through n. Then estimate implied volatility as of the end of periods one through n. Next estimate actual volatility in periods two through n plus one. Two simple linear regressions can then be performed— one in which the independent variable is the historical volatility and the dependent variable is the actual volatility in the subsequent period, and the other in which the independent variable is the implied volatility and the dependent variable is the actual volatility in the subsequent period.

It may be tempting to conclude that the regression equation with the higher R-squared reveals the better predictor, but this conclusion may very well be wrong. The regression equation with implied volatility as the independent variable may have a higher R-squared, but the slope of the regression line may be significantly greater or less than one, or the intercept may be significantly greater or less than zero. In these cases, the forecasts would be biased, although the R-squared alone would not reveal this. The regression equation with historical volatility as the independent variable might have the weaker R-squared but a slope and intercept closer to one and zero, respectively. In this contrived example, historical volatility may be the better predictor of subsequent volatility, even though it has a lower R-squared than implied volatility.[5]

An alternative method of comparison would be to examine the tracking errors associated with historical and implied volatilities. Tracking error is computed by squaring the differences between actual values and historical or implied values, taking the average of these differences, and then calculating the square root of the average.

A relatively recent innovation for estimating volatility uses a technique known as ARCH, an acronym for Autoregressive Conditional Heteroscedasticity.[6] Essentially, ARCH and related models incorporate the time-series dynamics of past volatility to forecast subsequent volatility. I discuss ARCH models in Chapter 13.

Notes

1. See, for example, Chapter 1.

2. To be precise, we should use the continuously compounded riskless rate of interest. Thus, if the rate is quoted as simple interest, we should use the natural log of one plus the interest rate.

3. For a discussion of the cumulative normal distribution function, see Chapter 2.

4. For an excellent review of this approach, see S. Brown, "Estimating Volatility," in Figlewski, Silber and Subrahmanyam, eds., *Financial Options: From Theory to Practice* (Homewood, IL: Business One Irwin, 1990).

5. For further elucidation, see L. Canina and S. Figlewski, "The Information Content of Implied Volatility" (Working paper number S-91-20, Salomon Center, New York University).

6. See R. Engle, "Autoregressive Conditional Heteroscedasticity with Estimates of the Variance of United Kingdom Inflation," *Econometrica* 17, pp. 5–26.

13

Estimating Volatility: Part 2

Choose the correct answer:

Autoregressive Conditional Heteroscedasticity (ARCH) is:

- a computer programming malfunction in which a variable is assigned more than one definition, causing the program to lock into an infinite loop;

- a psychological disorder characterized by a reversion to earlier behavior patterns when confronted with unpleasant childhood memories;

- in evolution, a reversion to a more primitive life form caused by inadequate diversity within a species;

- a statistical procedure in which the dependent variable in a regression equation is modeled as a function of the time-varying properties of the error term.

To the uninitiated, all the above definitions might seem equally plausible. Moreover, the correct definition, (4), may still not yield an intuitively satisfying description of ARCH.

This chapter is intended as a child's guide to ARCH, which is to say that it contains no equations. My goal is to penetrate the cryptic jargon of ARCH so that at the very least you will feel comfortable attending social events hosted by members of the American Association of Statisticians. Of course, you should not expect that familiarity with ARCH will actually cause you to have fun at such events.

Normal Assumptions of Volatility

In the preceding chapter, I reviewed two procedures for estimating volatility—one by which volatility is estimated directly from historical observations and an alternative procedure by which we infer volatility from the prices at which options on the underlying assets trade. One of the implicit assumptions of both these approaches is that volatility is stable.[1] Stability, in this context, does not suggest that volatility remains constant through time. Rather, it implies that volatility changes unpredictably, or that it is uncorrelated with previous levels of volatility.

For example, if we were to calculate the differences between monthly stock returns and their mean and regress the squared values of these differences (called the errors squared) in month t against their values in month t-1, we would not expect to detect a significant relationship. More specifically, the intercept of the regression line should be close to the average value of the errors squared, and the slope of the regression line should not differ significantly from zero.[2] Figure 13.1 represents this relationship impressionistically.

The parameters of the linear regression model depicted in Figure 13.1 would probably suggest that the errors squared are not autocorrelated, because the slope of the regression line is flat and the intercept seems close to the average value of the observations. We should not necessarily assume, however, that the errors squared are serially independent (uncorrelated with their prior values) simply because the regression parameters from a linear regression are insignificant. We must look further and examine the residuals around the fitted values.

The residuals equal the differences between the actual values for the errors squared and the values predicted from the regression line. If the errors squared were serially independent, the residuals would be distributed randomly around an expected value of zero. If the residuals satisfied this condition, we would describe them as *homoscedastic*.

Figure 13.1   Variance as a Function of Its Prior Values

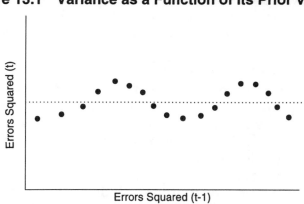

Errors Squared (t-1)

Nonlinearity

Suppose that high values for the errors squared occur in clusters. It might still be the case that the coefficients from the linear regression of the errors squared on their prior values are insignificant. If, however, the errors squared are related to their prior values in some nonlinear fashion, this nonlinear relationship might be revealed by the patterns formed by the residuals around the fitted values.

Reexamining Figure 13.1, for example, we notice that positive residuals (where the regression line underestimates the actual errors squared) tend to be followed by more positive residuals and that negative residuals appear in groups as well. We refer to such patterns in the residuals as *heteroscedasticity*.

We can correct for this apparent nonlinearity by regressing the residuals in period t on the errors squared in period t-1. We then add the intercept and slope from this regression equation to the intercept and slope from the original regression of the errors squared on their prior values. In effect, we conjecture that variance—the average value of the errors squared—is conditioned on this heteroscedasticity. This explains the term, *autoregressive conditional heteroscedasticity*.

The procedure is summarized below.

- Subtract the observed returns from their mean and square these differences to calculate the errors squared.

- Regress the errors squared in period t on the errors squared in period t-1.

- Subtract the fitted errors squared in period t from the observed errors squared in period t-1.

- Regress the residuals from step (3) in period t on the errors squared in period t-1.

- Add the intercept and slope from the regression equation in step (4) to the intercept and slope from the regression equation in step (2) to form a new prediction equation for variance.

The resulting equation should be a more efficient predictor of variance than the equation resulting from the original regression model of the errors squared on their prior values to the extent that the residuals from the original model are heteroscedastic. However, the process we have just described is not precisely the process that is used in an ARCH model.

Purists would recommend that one divide both the left-hand side and the right-hand side of the regression equation in step (4) by the fitted values for the errors squared from the regression equation in step (2). This is referred to as a generalized-least-squares method.[3]

Summary

Variance may be related to its past values. However, we may fail to detect this autoregressive relationship with a linear regression model of the errors squared if the relationship is nonlinear. If we have reason to suspect a nonlinear relationship, we should test the residuals between the actual values for the errors squared and the fitted values from an autoregressive equation for heteroscedasticity. If there is significant heteroscedasticity in the residuals, we should model the heteroscedasticity and incorporate it in our forecast equation for variance.

As one would expect, ARCH has spawned several other related procedures for modeling heteroscedasticity. We now have GARCH (Generalized ARCH), which includes lagged values for the dependent variable as well as the error term, and EGARCH (Exponential GARCH), which uses the logs of the variables. These are but two of several variations on the ARCH theme. As a contribution to the proliferation of ARCH-related acronyms, it is only fitting that I apply the acronym, PARCH, to the heuristic procedure described above; PARCH, of course, stands for "Poor man's ARCH."

Notes

1. Is this an oxymoron?

2. For a review of regression analysis, see Chapter 10.

3. For a more rigorous description of ARCH and related models see:

    Bollerslev, Tim, Ray Chou, Narayaman Jayaraman and Kenneth Kroner, "ARCH Modeling in Finance: A Selective Review of the Theory and Empirical Evidence, with Suggestions for Future Research" (Working paper presented at the UCSD

Conference on Modeling Volatility in Financial Markets, April 6–7, 1990);

Engle, Robert, "Autoregressive Conditional Heteroscedasticity with Estimates of the Variance of U.K. Inflation," *Econometrica* 50 (1982), pp. 987–1008; and

Greene, William H., *Econometric Analysis* (New York: MacMillan Publishing, 1990), pp. 416–419.

14
Hypothesis Testing

Financial analysts work with noisy data. As a consequence, it is often difficult to determine whether observed results are due to a real effect or reside within the realm of noise. This chapter reviews the methodology referred to as hypothesis testing to distinguish real effects from noise.

Hypothesis Test for Comparing Proportions from a Small Sample

Suppose we wish to test whether or not a coin is fair. We begin by defining the null hypothesis and the alternative hypothesis. In this example, the null hypothesis, denoted by H_o, is that the coin is fair. The alternative hypothesis, denoted by H_a, is that the coin is biased.

Next we need to compute a test statistic. We do so by repeatedly tossing the coin and observing how often it comes up heads and how often it comes up tails.

Finally, we need to compute a P value, which is the probability that the test statistic would occur if the null hypothesis were true. The estimation of the P value depends on the notion of a Bernoulli trial.

A Bernoulli trial has three properties. Its result must be characterized by a success or a failure. The probability of a success must be the same for all of the trials. The outcome of each trial must be independent of the outcomes of the other trials. The toss of a coin clearly satisfies the conditions of a Bernoulli trial.

The fraction of successes from a sequence of Bernoulli trials is called a binomial random variable and serves as the test statistic in this example. The P value, which is the probability of observing a particular test statistic from a binomial distribution, is given by equation (1).

$$P(X) = \frac{n!}{X! \, (n - X)!} \, p^X \, (1 - p)^{n - X} \qquad (1)$$

where

P(X) = probability of X heads in n tosses,

   n = number of tosses in the sample,

   p = expected proportion of heads resulting from
          tossing a fair coin,

   X = number of heads observed in the sample and

   ! = factorial (for example, $5! = 5 \times 4 \times 3 \times 2 \times 1$)

Suppose we toss the coin 10 times and observe eight heads. In our example, n equals 10, p equals 0.50, and X equals eight. If we substitute these values into equation (1), we find that there is only a 4.39 percent probability of observing eight heads in 10 tosses. The probability of observing nine heads equals 0.98 percent and the probability of observing 10 heads equals 0.10 percent. Thus the probability of observing eight or more heads equals 5.47%. By symmetry, the probability of observing two or fewer heads also equals 5.47%. Thus there is a 10.94% chance of observing eight or more or two or fewer heads given a fair coin. If we require 95% confidence, we would fail to reject the null hypothesis that the coin is fair.

It is important to note that we can never accept the null hypothesis. We can reject the null hypothesis or we can fail to reject the null hypothesis. This is the only term with which I am familiar that constitutes a triple negative. In the event we fail to reject the null hypothesis, we conclude that the test lacks sufficient power to accept the alternative hypothesis.

Hypothesis Test for Comparing Proportions from a Large Sample

Now let us explore an investment example. Suppose we are evaluating an equity portfolio manager who claims she can identify companies that are likely to be takeover targets, and we arrive at a mutually acceptable definition of a takeover target. At the end of a one-year measurement period we observe that 10 percent of the companies in her portfolio were the target of takeover attempts. Should we attribute this result to her skill or to chance?

In this example the null hypothesis is that the fraction of takeover targets in her portfolio was due purely to chance. The alternative hypothesis is that she is skillful in selecting takeover targets. In order to test which hypothesis is true, we again need to develop a test statistic to weigh the evidence.

We proceed as follows. We first compute the fraction of companies that were takeover targets in the entire universe of stocks from which she selected her portfolio. Suppose that there are 5,000 companies in the universe and 7 percent of them were takeover targets during the period for which she is being evaluated.

Moreover suppose that there were no commonalties among them to suggest that a particular type of company was more likely than other companies to be a takeover target. Hence we conclude that each company in the universe has the same 7 percent probability of being a takeover target.

Finally, assume that each remaining company's chance of being a takeover target is independent of the status of the companies already selected. This assumption is not literally true. When the portfolio manager selects companies for her portfolio, she slightly changes the odds that the remaining companies in the universe are takeover targets. Because the universe is so large and her sample is relatively small, however, the effect is negligible.

The process of selecting a company from a universe and determining whether or not it turns out to be a takeover target is a Bernoulli trial. Thus the fraction of takeover targets in her portfolio is a binomial random variable.

In this example, we are dealing with a relatively large sample (100 companies versus 10 coin tosses). With a large sample size, we can use the normal distribution to approximate the binomial distribution. As a rule of thumb, we can use the normal distribution to estimate the P value (probability of rejecting the null hypothesis when it is true) as long as both the sample size multiplied by the fraction of successes and the sample size multiplied by the quantity, one minus the fraction of successes, are greater than five. This condition is satisfied in this example because the products of 100 times 0.10 and 100 times 0.90 both exceed five.

Again we must compute a test statistic to measure how far the proportion of takeover targets in her portfolio differs from the proportion of takeover targets in the universe. The appropriate test statistic is given by equation (2).

$$z = \frac{p_p - p_u}{\sqrt{p_u (1 - p_u)/n}} \qquad (2)$$

where

p_p = proportion of companies in her portfolio that were takeover targets,

p_u = proportion of companies in the universe that were takeover targets and

n = number of stocks in her portfolio

The term $p_u(1 - p_u)$ equals the variance of the proportion of takeover targets in the universe.

In our example, the test statistic z equals 1.18. If we look this value up in a normal distribution table, we find that there is a 12 percent chance that her success rate would occur even if the null hypothesis were true. Thus if we wished to be 95 percent confident, we would fail to reject the null hypothesis and conclude instead that the hypothesis test lacks sufficient power to detect her potential skill.

For a 5 percent or lower probability of rejecting the null hypothesis when it is true, the test statistic for a normal distribution must equal or exceed 1.645, assuming the portfolio manager does not have negative skill. This type of test is called a right-handed test because we base our rejection of the null hypothesis on whether or not the area under the normal distribution curve to the right of the test statistic is greater than or equal to our prechosen threshold (5 percent in this example).

With simple algebra, we can determine how many takeover targets, expressed as a fraction of the number of stocks in her portfolio, she would have to identify before we should accept the alternative hypothesis that she is skillful. This formula is given by equation (3).

$$p_p = p_u + z \cdot \sqrt{p_u(1 - p_u)/n} \qquad (3)$$

Based on a portfolio of 100 stocks and the fact that 7 percent of the companies in the universe from which she chose her portfolio were takeover targets, 11.2 percent of the companies in her portfolio must be takeover targets before we should characterize her as skillful.

Hypothesis Test for Large Sample Means

In the previous example, we used the binomial distribution as approximated by the normal distribution to test the hypothesis that the proportion of takeover targets in a particular portfolio was significantly greater than the proportion of takeover targets in the universe from which the portfolio was selected. Next we test the hypothesis that the value of the yen has trended up relative to the dollar from the beginning of 1994 through March 31, 1994.

In this example, the null hypothesis is that the slope of yen's return relative to the dollar for the first quarter of 1994 was flat or negative. The alternative hypothesis is that the yen relative to the dollar had a positive slope during the first quarter.

We assume that the natural logarithms of exchange rates are normally distributed. Therefore, the test statistic is computed as follows.

$$z = \frac{X - \mu}{s/\sqrt{n}} \qquad (4)$$

where,

X = mean of daily yen continuous returns,

μ = 0 percent daily return (corresponding to a flat slope),

s = standard deviation of daily yen continuous returns and

n = number of daily returns in the sample measurement period

The mean of the daily yen continuous returns was 0.13 percent, and the standard deviation of these returns was 0.66 percent. Because there were 71 daily returns in the first quarter of 1994, the z value equals 1.66, which corresponds to slightly less than a 5 percent probability of rejecting the null hypothesis when it is true. In other words, we are a little more than 95 percent confident that the return of the yen sloped upward during the first quarter of 1994.

This test is also a right-handed test because we are interested in the probability that the yen's slope is greater than zero.

Suppose instead that we wish to test whether the yen sloped *either* up or down. We are interested in the probability that the yen's slope is *different* from zero—that it merely trended. Tests aimed at establishing this are called two-sided. If we require 95 percent confidence to reject the null hypothesis, the critical value is 1.96 rather than 1.645. Thus, in the above example we fail to reject the null hypotheses that the yen's slope was zero rather than accept the alternative hypothesis that the slope was different from zero. A two-sided test in this example is more reasonable, because we have no reason to believe that the yen necessarily cannot trend down.

Hypothesis Tests for Small Sample Means

In the preceding example our sample of daily returns consisted of 71 observations. With 71 observations it is usually safe to assume that the data are approximately normally distributed, as long as the distribution of the underlying population is normally distributed. In situations where we have smaller samples, however, we should account for sampling error. Sampling error widens the distribution, which simply means that with fewer observations we are less confident in the result than we would be had we obtained the result from a larger sample. The extent to which the distribution should be widened was first estimated by William Gosset, an employee of the Guiness Brewery. Gosset published his findings under the pseudonym, Student. The test statistic is called the t statistic, and it is calculated as shown in equation (5).

$$t = \frac{X - \mu}{s/\sqrt{n}} \qquad (5)$$

The t statistic is calculated the same way as the z value except that we assume that the sample standard deviation is different from the population standard deviation. In the previous example, I assumed implicitly that the sample standard deviation and the population standard deviation were the same or sufficiently close not to matter. For large samples, this assumption is harmless. For small samples, we correct for the difference between the observed sample standard deviation and the unobserved population standard deviation by using a t table instead of a normal distribution table.

A t table requires us to specify the degrees of freedom in our sample. It equals the number of observations in the sample less one. We must subtract one because we use up one degree of freedom in estimating the mean. Table 14.1 shows the t-statistics required to reject the null hypothesis at the 5 percent level for various sample sizes based on a right-handed test. This means there is only a 5 percent chance of rejecting the null hypothesis when it is true. These values should be compared with a z value equal to 1.645 for a normal distribution.

Table 14.1 t-Statistic Required for 5 Percent Error of Rejecting Null Hypothesis When It Is True

Degrees of Freedom	t-Statistic
1	6.31
2	2.92
3	2.35
4	2.13
5	2.01
10	1.81
20	1.72
50	1.68
100	1.66

It should be intuitively satisfying that for the same level of confidence, the t statistic is greater than the z value, and that as the sample size increases, the required t statistic approaches the required z value.

Now let us consider a small sample problem. Suppose we simulate an investment strategy over a five-year measurement period and produce quarterly returns in excess of the benchmark that average 1.5 percent with a quarterly standard deviation in excess of the benchmark of 3.6 percent. We wish to determine whether or not this strategy adds value to the benchmark. The null hypothesis is that the strategy adds no value, while the alternative hypothesis is that the strategy adds value. (Again, I assume there is no negative skill.)

The t-statistic in this example equals 1.86, as shown below.

$$1.86 = \frac{1.5\% - 0\%}{3.6\% / \sqrt{20}}$$

There are 19 degrees of freedom. In order to reject the null hypothesis that the strategy adds no value or equivalently that 1.5 percent is not positive relative to the benchmark, the t-statistic must equal or exceed 1.73, assuming our tolerance for error is 5 percent. Thus we reject the null hypothesis that the strategy does not add value.

If this result were instead obtained over 12 quarters, the t-statistic would equal 1.44, and we would fail to reject the null hypothesis. We see, therefore, that the size of the sample increases our confidence in the result, given the same sample mean and standard deviation.

Type I Error versus Type II Error

The hypothesis tests that I have thus far described test for a *Type I error*, which occurs when we reject a null hypothesis that is actually true.

A *Type II error*, by contrast, occurs when we fail to reject a null hypothesis that is false; that is, when the alternative hypothesis is true.

Suppose the null hypothesis is that a money manager is not skillful, and the alternative hypothesis is that the money manager is skillful.

Table 14.2 distinguishes a Type I error from a Type II error.

The probability of a Type I error is simply the probability of rejecting the null hypothesis when it is true. It is the area under the t distribution or normal distribution to the right and/or left of the test statistic.

The probability of a Type II error depends on the test statistic we choose to reject the null hypothesis and our assumption about the unobservable population mean.

Suppose, for example, we wish to evaluate a portfolio manager. The null hypothesis is that the manager will not add value, and the alternative hypothesis is that he will. We intend to hire the manager if we are at least 95 percent confident he has skill. We will not hire him, however, if our doubt about his skill exceeds 5 percent. Our sample includes 10 years of monthly excess returns with a mean of 0.25 percent and a standard deviation of 2.00 percent. We thus compute the z value as:

$$1.37 = \frac{.25\% - 0.00\%}{2.00\%/\sqrt{120}}$$

Table 14.2 Type I Error versus Type II Error
Null Hypothesis: Manager Is Not Skillful

Belief	Truth	
	Manager Is Not Skillful	Manager Is Skillful
Manager Is Not Skillful	No Error	Type II Error
Manager Is Skillful	Type I Error	No Error

This value corresponds to a 9 percent chance of hiring a manager that has no skill. Given our 5 percent standard, therefore, we should not hire this manager.

The probability of a Type II error measures the likelihood that we do not hire a skillful manager. We compute this probability by first computing the mean return that would be necessary to reject the null hypothesis that the manager has no skill. The 5 percent cutoff that we have chosen corresponds to a z value of 1.645. Thus we require a return that is 1.645 standard deviations (adjusted for sample size) above the null hypothesis return of 0 percent. We compute this value as:

$$0.30\% = 1.645 \times 2.00\%/\sqrt{120}$$

Next we compute a z value to measure the distance between this required return and our assumed unobservable future return. Suppose the unobservable future return is the same as the manager's sample return. The z value, therefore, equals:

$$0.27 = \frac{0.30\% - 0.25\%}{2.00\%/\sqrt{120}}$$

This z value implies that there is a 61 percent chance that we will fail to hire a skillful manager. The *power of this test* is measured by the quantity 1 minus the probability of a Type II error.

It, therefore, equals the probability of rejecting the null hypothesis when it is false. In this example it refers to the likelihood that the test will lead us to hire a skillful manager. Its value equals 39 percent.

Suppose that after contemplating the tradeoff between not hiring a manager with no skill and failing to hire a manager with skill, we conclude that our 5 percent standard for rejecting the null hypothesis is too strict. We decide to relax it such that we will tolerate a 10 percent chance of hiring a manager who really has no skill. (I suspect very few managers would be hired otherwise.) The new z value equals 1.28; hence, we should now hire the manager.

What is the likelihood, given our new 10 percent standard, that we will hire a manager with no skill if we still assume that the unobservable future return equals 0.25%?

We must compute the required return associated with a 1.28 z value. It equals 0.23 percent. Then we compute the z value for the difference between the required return and our assumption about the future unobservable return. It equals -0.09, which corresponds to a 46 percent chance of hiring a manager with no skill and a 54 percent chance of hiring a skillful manager.

The tradeoff between a Type I error and a Type II error is as follows. The stricter we are in avoiding a Type I error (in order not to hire a manager without skill), the more likely it is that we will commit a Type II error (that is, fail to hire a skillful manager), and by symmetry, the weaker will be the power of our test.

The choice of the appropriate threshold for rejecting the null hypothesis depends on the importance we assign to avoiding a Type I error relative to the importance we assign to avoiding a Type II error.

15
Monte Carlo Simulation

As financial analysts, we are often required to anticipate the future. Monte Carlo simulation is a numerical technique that allows us to experience the future with the aid of a computer. This chapter reviews some of the important concepts that are relevant to Monte Carlo simulation and describes the procedures one would undertake to perform such a simulation.

Deterministic versus Stochastic Models

In order to forecast the future, we build models that define the relationship between a set of inputs and a description of the future. Models that assume a fixed relationship between the inputs and the output are called *deterministic;* the inputs lead unambiguously to the answer. Models that depend on inputs that are influenced by chance or estimated with uncertainty are called *stochastic*. Stochastic models do not yield unambiguous solutions; instead, they provide a *distribution* of probable answers.

A model that predicts an eclipse, for example, is deterministic, because it relies on known fixed laws governing the motions of the earth, the moon and the sun. You are unlikely to hear an astronomer say there is a 30 percent chance of an eclipse next Wednesday. A model that predicts tomorrow's weather, however, is stochastic, because many uncertain elements influence the weather.

A variable that is influenced by chance is called a random variable. In a deterministic model, we assign a single value to a variable; in a stochastic model, we assign a distribution of probable values to a random variable. We often represent the random variable's distribution by its mean and standard deviation.

We solve deterministic models analytically, which simply means that we represent the model with a mathematical formula and then solve the formula. Many stochastic models can also be solved analytically. It is sometimes inefficient or not possible to solve a stochastic model analytically, however. In such a case, we must resort to a numerical solution.

To solve a model numerically, we try out various values for the model's parameters and variables. When the values we use are a succession of random numbers, the numerical solution is called a Monte Carlo simulation.

The term Monte Carlo simulation was introduced by John von Neumann and Stanislaw Ulam when they both worked on the Manhattan Project at the Los Alamos National Laboratory. Ulam invented the procedure of substituting a sequence of random numbers into equations to solve problems relating to the physics of nuclear explosions. The two of them used the term as a code name for the secret work they were conducting.[1] The choice of the name was obviously inspired by the gambling casinos in Monte Carlo.

Random Numbers

In order to perform a Monte Carlo simulation, we need access to a sequence of numbers that are distributed uniformly and are independent of each other. Ideally, the numbers should be random. Unfortunately, truly random numbers are almost impossible to obtain except by some mechanical process that is typically costly or time-consuming. We could generate random numbers by rolling dice and recording the results, for example, but we would probably tire long before we had a sufficiently long sequence of numbers. Moreover, the dice might have a slight, undetectable bias.

As an alternative to mechanically generated random numbers, we can use mathematical techniques to generate pseudorandom numbers. We might start by squaring the last four digits of our phone number. Then we could extract the middle four digits and proceed by squaring the middle four digits we just extracted and extracting the middle four digits from the new squared value. We could continue in this manner for as long as necessary or until the middle four digits contain a sequence of zeros that terminates the process.

This approach, invented by John von Neumann, is called the mid-square method.[2] The sequence of numbers it generates are called pseudorandom numbers because they come from a purely deterministic process. As long as they are uniform and independent, however, they will suffice for most Monte Carlo simulations. By *uniform* we mean that all the numbers have an equal chance of occurrence. Independence implies that the numbers are unrelated to one another.

There are many methods for generating pseudorandom numbers that are independent and uniformly distributed. Most statistics packages and spreadsheet software include random-number generators.

In many financial analysis applications, the random variables of interest are not distributed uniformly; rather, they conform to some other distribution. In order to perform a Monte Carlo simulation of a model in which the random variables are normally distributed, we must transform our sequence of uniformly distributed random numbers into a sequence of normally distributed random numbers.

Monte Carlo Simulation of the Stock Market

Suppose we allocate $100,000 to an S&P 500 index fund in which the dividends are reinvested, and we wish to forecast the value of our investment 10 years from now. We can start by generating a series of 10 random numbers that are uniformly distributed within the range of zero to one. We assume, however, that the S&P's returns are normally distributed.[3] Hence we need to transform our uniform sequence into a random sequence that is normally distributed.[4]

There is a convenient way to accomplish this transformation. According to the Central Limit Theorem, if we sum or average a group of independent random variables, which themselves are not normally distributed, the sum or average will be normally distributed if the group is sufficiently large. Most advanced statistics books contain a proof of this important theorem. For those who do not require a formal proof, I will provide a simple intuitive demonstration.

Suppose the value of a random variable, X, is determined by the toss of a fair die. There is a one-in-six chance that X will take on the value 1, a one-in-six chance that it will take on the value 2, and the same chance that it will take on the value 3, 4, 5 or 6. Clearly, X is uniformly distributed because there is an equal probability of experiencing each outcome, and its values are independent because they are determined purely by chance. Now consider a second random variable, Y, whose value is determined by the toss of another die. Y has the same uniform distribution as X, although their outcomes are independent of one another.

Now consider a third random variable—the average of the values of X and Y. The distribution of the third random variable, called $(X + Y)/2$, is not uniform. There is a greater likelihood it will take on a value close to 3 or 4 than one close to 1 or 6. The obvious reason is that there are more ways to experience a 3 or a 4 than there are a 1 or a 6. Table 15.1 shows the relative frequencies of the values for each of the three random variables.

The relative frequencies for the random variable (X + Y)/2 are computed by summing the probabilities for all the combinations of X and Y that yield the relevant average value. For example, there is a 5/36 chance that the random variable (X + Y)/2 will take on the value 3, because there are five combinations of X and Y whose average equals 3, each of which has a 1/36 chance of occurrence: X = 1 and Y = 5; X = 5 and Y = 1; X = 2 and Y = 4; X = 4 and Y = 2; and X = 3 and Y = 3.

It is easy to see from Table 15.1 that although neither X nor Y individually is normally distributed, their sum or average begins to approach a normal distribution. This result suggests that we can generate a sequence of random numbers that is normally distributed by combining sequences of random numbers that are uniformly distributed.

The algorithm that gives the best estimate of a random number drawn from a normal distribution is given below:

$$X_n = \left(\sum_{i=1}^{n} U_i - n/2 \right) \cdot \frac{1}{\sqrt{n/12}}$$

Table 15.1 Demonstration of the Central Limit Theorem

	Relative Frequencies		
Value	X	Y	(X + Y)/2
1.0	1/6	1/6	1/36
1.5	0	0	2/36
2.0	1/6	1/6	3/36
2.5	0	0	4/36
3.0	1/6	1/6	5/36
3.5	0	0	6/36
4.0	1/6	1/6	5/36
4.5	0	0	4/36
5.0	1/6	1/6	3/36
5.5	0	0	2/36
6.0	1/6	1/6	1/36

where
  X_n = Estimate of random number drawn from a normal distribution with a mean of 0 and a standard deviation of 1.
  U_i = Random number drawn from a uniform distribution.
  n = number of random numbers drawn from a uniform distribution.

Table 15.2 shows two sequences of random numbers. The first sequence is uniformly distributed between the values 0 and 1. The second sequence is comprised of estimated values assumed to be drawn from a normal distribution with a mean of 0 and a standard deviation of 1.[5] Although we now have a sequence of random numbers that is normally distributed, we are not yet ready to simulate the performance of our investment in the S&P 500 index fund. In order to proceed, we should rescale our normally distributed sequence to reflect our views about the mean return and standard deviation of the S&P 500. Suppose we believe that the average return of the S&P 500 is 12 percent and that its standard deviation is 20 percent. We rescale our standardized normal sequence by multiplying each observation by our assumption for the S&P's standard deviation and adding to this value our assumption for its average return. Now we have a sequence of returns that we can use to simulate our investment's performance. Table 15.3 gives this sequence.

In order to carry out the simulation, we simply link the sequence of random returns and multiply this result by 100,000 to derive an

Table 15.2 Random Numbers	
Uniform Sequence	**Normal Sequence**
.6471	−.7285
.4162	.1451
.5691	.2131
.2006	−1.1258
.4685	1.8016
.7442	.2572
.9439	−1.2093
.5556	−.2718
.2480	−1.1153
.3644	1.7516

Table 15.3 Rescaling a Normally Distributed Sequence

	A 0,1 **Normally Distributed Sequence**	B A · .20	C B + .12
	−.7285	−.1457	−.0257
	.1451	.0290	.1490
	.2131	.0426	.1626
	−1.1258	−.2252	−.1052
	1.8016	.3603	.4803
	.2572	.0514	.1714
	−1.2093	−.2419	−.1219
	−.2718	−.0544	.0656
	−1.1153	−.2231	−.1031
	1.7516	.3503	.4703
Average	−.0282	−.0056	.1144
Standard Deviation	1.0496	.2099	.2099

estimate of our investment's value 10 years forward. The simulated returns in column C of Table 15.3, for example, yield a terminal value of $249,252.

We repeat the entire process beginning with the step in which we generate the random numbers from a uniform distribution. We proceed as described until we generate a sufficiently large number of estimates. The distribution of these estimates is the solution to our problem. Figure 15.1 illustrates a frequency distribution of the terminal value of $100,000, 10 years hence, resulting from 100 simulations performed as I have just described.

From this information, we can estimate the likelihood that our fund's value will equal or exceed various wealth goals. We simply count the relative frequency of outcomes above or below the value we are interested in.

Simulation versus Analytical Solution

The example I have just described is intended to illustrate the steps one would take to perform a Monte Carlo simulation. There is noth-

Figure 15.1 Frequency Distribution for $100,000 10 Years Forward Based on 100 Simulations

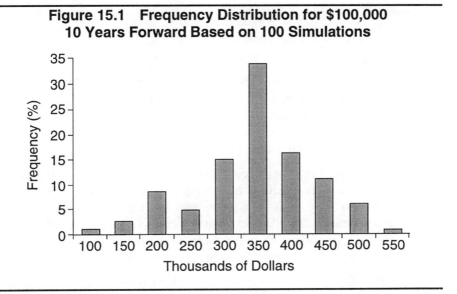

ing about this particular problem that prevents us from solving it analytically. Given the assumptions that the S&P's returns are random and normally distributed, we can simply calculate the normal deviate associated with alternative values for terminal wealth and find the corresponding probability of achieving that value in a normal distribution table.[6]

There are many problems, however, that are more amenable to a Monte Carlo simulation than to an analytical solution. Suppose, for example, that we plan to contribute half of our investment's return each year to our favorite charity. It is considerably easier to simulate our investment's growth after accounting for these conditional disbursements than it would be to devise an analytical solution. We simply reduce our fund's value each year in each simulation by half of the fund's randomly generated return. Try to figure out an analytical solution to this problem.

Monte Carlo simulation is a valuable tool for forecasting events, especially for problems that are too complex to be described by equations. It is important, however, to repeat the simulation enough times to obtain a reliable result.

Notes

1. M. Browne, "Coin-Tossing Computers Found to Show Subtle Bias," *New York Times*, January 12, 1993.

2. R. Rubenstein, *Simulation and the Monte Carlo Method* (New York: John Wiley & Sons, Inc., 1981), pp. 20-21. This book also describes more advanced methods for generating pseudorandom numbers. Moreover it is an excellent resource for those who wish to pursue this topic.

3. Actually, it is more acceptable to assume that the logarithms of the wealth relatives of the S&P's returns are normally distributed. The returns themselves are usually assumed to be lognormally distributed. If we were to use the logarithms of the wealth relatives, we would sum them and then take the anti-log of the sum to determine terminal wealth.

4. The 10 numbers selected from the uniform distribution are not themselves perfectly uniformly distributed because they comprise too small a sample. Nor, for the same reason, will the 10 transformed numbers be perfectly normally distributed. Thus, when I describe a sequence of 10 numbers as uniformally or normally distributed, I mean that they are drawn from respective distributions with uniform or normal distributions.

5. The uniformly distributed random sequences were generated by using the @rand function in Lotus123.

6. For a review of this analytical approach, see Chapter 2.

16
Future Value

Suppose we want to estimate the future value of an investment based on its return history. This problem, at first glance, might seem pedestrian. Yet it involves subtleties that confound many financial analysts.

Some analysts argue that the best guide for estimating future value is the arithmetic average of past returns. Others claim that the geometric average provides a better estimate of future value. The correct answer depends on what it is about future value that we want to estimate.

Averages

Let us proceed with a quick review of the geometric average. The geometric average is calculated by adding 1 to the holding-period returns, multiplying these values together, raising the product to the power of 1 divided by the number of returns, and then subtracting 1. It is sometimes called the constant rate of return or the annualized return.

We can also compute the geometric average by converting holding-period returns into continuous returns. A continuous return, when compounded continuously, yields the same wealth we would achieve by investing at the holding-period return. It equals the natural logarithm of the quantity 1 plus the holding-period return. If the holding-period return equals 10 percent, for example, the continuous return equals 9.53 percent. If we were to invest $1.00 at an annual rate of 9.53 percent compounded continuously throughout the year, it would grow to $1.10 by the end of the year.

We calculate the geometric average from continuous returns by raising e (2.7182), the base of the natural logarithm, to the power of the arithmetic average of the continuous returns and subtracting 1.

Table 16.1 shows how to compute the arithmetic and geometric averages. We compute the arithmetic average by summing the values in the first column and dividing by 4. It equals 8.00 percent. We can compute the geometric average in two ways. We can multiply the values in the second column, which yields 1.3206, then take the fourth root of 1.3206 and subtract 1 to arrive at the geometric average, 7.20 percent. Alternatively, we can compute the arithmetic average of the third column, raise e to this value, and subtract 1 to arrive again at 7.20 percent. It follows, therefore, that the arithmetic average of the logarithms of the quantities 1 plus the holding-period returns equals the logarithm of the quantity 1 plus the geometric average.

Here is how to interpret the geometric average. If we invest $1.00 in this sequence of returns, our dollar will grow to $1.3206. We would achieve the same terminal value by investing $1.00 at a constant rate of 7.20 percent for the four periods.

Expected Value

Now consider our earlier question. Which average should we use to estimate future value, assuming we wish to base our estimate on past returns? The question as I have posed it is too vague. We must be more precise about what we wish to know about future value. If our goal is to estimate an investment's expected value either one period forward or many periods forward, we should use the arithmetic average of holding-period returns. We estimate expected value from past returns by adding 1 to this average and compounding this quantity forward.

Table 16.1 Averages

Arithmetic Holding-Period Return (HPR)		Geometric 1+HPR		Geometric ln(1+HPR)
12.00%		1.1200		11.33%
−6.00		0.9400		−6.19
28.00		1.2800		24.69
−2.00		0.9800		−2.02
Sum: 32.00	Product:	1.3206	Sum:	27.81
Average: 8.00	4th Root−1:	7.20%	Average:	6.95
			Exponential−1:	7.20

In order to see why the arithmetic average is used to estimate expected value, consider an investment that has a 50 percent chance of increasing by 25 percent and a 50 percent chance of decreasing by 5 percent. After one period, there is an even chance that a dollar will grow to $1.25 or decline to $0.95. The expected value after one period thus equals $1.10, which in turn equals 1 plus the arithmetic average of the two possible returns. After two periods, there are four equally likely outcomes. The investment can increase to $1.25 after the first period and then increase to $1.5625 the second period or decrease to $1.1875. It can first decrease to $0.95 after the first period and then increase to $1.1875 or decrease further to $0.9025. Figure 16.1 diagrams these four possible paths.

The expected value after two periods, which equals the probability-weighted outcome, equals 1.2100. It corresponds precisely to the quantity 1 plus the arithmetic average of 10 percent raised to the second power. The geometric average of a 25 percent increase followed by a 5 percent decrease or a 5 percent decrease followed by a 25 percent increase equals 8.9725 percent. If we add 1 to the geometric average and compound it forward for two periods, we arrive at a terminal value of 1.1875, which does not equal the expected value. *The expected value is higher than the value we would have achieved had we invested in the returns on which the arithmetic average is based.*

This result might seem paradoxical. The intuition is as follows. The expected value assumes that there is an equal chance of experiencing any of the possible paths. A path of high returns raises the expected value over multiple periods more than a path of equal-magnitude

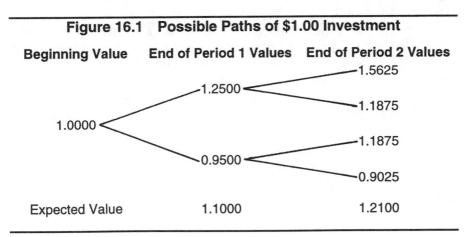

Figure 16.1 Possible Paths of $1.00 Investment

Beginning Value	End of Period 1 Values	End of Period 2 Values
		1.5625
	1.2500	
		1.1875
1.0000		
		1.1875
	0.9500	
		0.9025
Expected Value	1.1000	1.2100

low returns lowers it. This disproportionate effect is the result of compounding. Suppose the high return is 10 percent while the low return is -10 percent. Two consecutive high returns produce a 21 percent increase in value, while two consecutive low returns produce a decrease in value of only 19 percent.[1]

Here's how to interpret expected value. Suppose we observe 10 years of monthly returns and wish to estimate how much wealth we should expect to achieve if we were to draw randomly from these 120 monthly returns, *replacing each of the returns that is drawn.* If we were to invest in the 120 returns that we selected from the sample (without yet observing them), we should expect our investment to grow at a rate equal to the quantity 1 plus the arithmetic average of the sample of monthly returns, raised to the 120th power minus 1 or, equivalently, 1 plus the arithmetic average of the yearly returns from the sample, raised to the 10th power minus 1.

If we were to repeat this experiment many times, the average of the cumulative wealth generated from the sequences of randomly selected returns would indeed converge to the wealth predicted by the compounded arithmetic average. You can verify this result with a random-number generator.

Distribution of Future Value

Suppose we ask the following questions about future value. What is the likelihood or probability that an investment will grow or fall to a particular value? Or what value should we be 50 percent confident of achieving or failing to achieve? The answers to these questions depend on the geometric average.

Let's start with the assumption that the logarithms of the quantities 1 plus the holding-period returns are normally distributed.[2] This assumption implies that the returns themselves are lognormally distributed. It follows that the normal deviate used to estimate the probability of achieving a particular future value is calculated from the mean (arithmetic average) and standard deviation of these logarithms.[3]

A normal deviate measures distance from the mean in standard deviation units. It is the number that we look up in a normal distribution table to estimate the probability of achieving or falling short of a particular value.

Suppose we wish to estimate the likelihood that $1 million will grow to equal $1.5 million over five years, based on the past annual returns of a particular investment. If we believe that the logarithms of the quantities 1 plus these returns are normally distributed, we can proceed by computing the mean and standard deviation of these logarithms, as Table 16.2 shows.

We compute the normal deviate as follows:

$$Z = \frac{\ln(1{,}500{,}000/1{,}000{,}000) - 0.064695 \cdot 5}{0.108744 \cdot \sqrt{5}}$$

$$Z = 0.3372$$

The logarithm of the quantity 1.5 million divided by 1 million (40.5465%) is the continuous five-year return required in order for $1 million to grow to $1.5 million. It corresponds to an annualized continuous growth rate of 8.1093 percent. The quantity 5 times 6.4695 percent is the expected five-year continuous return. The normal deviate measures how far away the required five-year continuous return is from the expected five-year continuous return. It is 0.3372 standard-deviation units away. If we look up this value in a normal distribution table, we see that there is a 38.6 percent chance that $1 million will grow to $1.5 million, based on the past returns of this investment.

Table 16.2 Past Investment Returns

	Annual Return	In(1 + Return)
	−3.0200%	−3.0665%
	6.9500	6.7191
	27.1500	24.0197
	12.2700	11.5736
	−9.1400	−9.5850
	17.3000	15.9565
	2.1900	2.1664
	5.6500	5.4962
	−7.9100	−8.2404
	21.7200	19.6553
Arithmetic Average	7.3160	6.4695
Standard Deviation	11.6779	10.8744

Suppose we wish to know the likelihood that our investment will generate a loss over five years. We compute the normal deviate as:

$$Z = \frac{\ln(1{,}000{,}000/1{,}000{,}000) - 0.064695 \cdot 5}{0.108744 \cdot \sqrt{5}}$$

$$Z = -1.3303$$

There is a 9.17 percent chance that this investment will lose money, on average, over five years.

What value should we expect to equal or exceed with 50 percent confidence? This value is called the median. Half the values are expected to exceed the median and half are expected to fall short of the median. A 50 percent probability of occurrence corresponds to a normal deviate of 0.00. The normal deviate equals 0.00 only when the required continuous return equals the expected continuous return. Thus we should expect with 50 percent confidence to equal or exceed the value that corresponds to the expected five-year continuous return. We find this value by raising e, the base of the natural logarithm, to the power 5 times the expected annualized continuous return. Thus the median wealth equals $1,381,924.26. There is a 50 percent chance that the value in five years will exceed this value and a 50 percent chance that it will fall short of this value.

The geometric average is relevant for estimating probabilities, because the average of the logarithms equals the logarithm of the quantity 1 plus the geometric average.

The center of the probability distribution of terminal values is found by compounding the initial value at the geometric average. When we compound at the geometric average, we determine the future value for which there is an equal chance of exceeding or failing to exceed. Here is the logic behind this result.

- The logarithms of the quantities 1 plus the holding-period returns are assumed to be normally distributed.

- The mean (arithmetic average) of these logarithms equals the logarithm of the quantity 1 plus the geometric average of the holding-period returns.

- The expected multiperiod continuous return, therefore, equals the number of periods times the logarithm of the quantity 1 plus the geometric average.

- We convert the expected multiperiod continuous return into median wealth by raising e to the power of the multiperiod continuous return.

- The quantity e raised to the power of the multiperiod continuous return is exactly equal to the initial wealth compounded forward at the geometric average.

The bottom line is that we should compound at the *arithmetic* average if we wish to estimate an investment's expected value. We should compound at the *geometric* average, however, if we wish to estimate the likelihood that an investment will exceed or fall below a target value.

Some Formulas for Estimating Future Value

Here are some formulas that you should carry on your person at all times in the event you are called upon to discuss future value.

Expected future value is calculated as:

$$EV = B (1 + Ra)^n \qquad (1)$$

or

$$EV = Be^{(Rc + S^2/2)n} \qquad (2)$$

Median future value is calculated as:

$$MV = B (1 + Rg)^n \qquad (3)$$

or

$$MV = Be^{Rc(n)} \qquad (4)$$

The normal deviate for estimating the probability of achieving a target future value is:

$$Z = \frac{\ln(T/B) - \ln(1 + Rg)n}{S\sqrt{n}} \qquad (5)$$

In these formulas:

B = beginning value,
T = target value,
Ra = arithmetic average of holding-period returns,
Rg = geometric average of holding-period returns,

Rc = arithmetic average of the logarithms of the quantities 1
          plus the holding-period returns,
S = standard deviation of the logarithms of the quantities 1
          plus the holding-period returns,
e = base of the natural logarithm, 2.7128,
ln = natural logarithm and
n = number of periods.

When deciding whether to compound at the arithmetic average to estimate expected value or the geometric average to estimate the distribution of future value, you should be aware of the following distinction. More often than not, an investment will fail to achieve or exceed its expected value (compounded arithmetic average), which in some sense implies that the expected value is not to be expected.[4] Because of the effect of compounding, however, the fewer outcomes that exceed the expected value have a greater impact, *per outcome*, than the more frequent outcomes that fall below the expected value.

Half the outcomes should exceed the median value (compound geometric average) and half should fall below this value. Those values that are above the median, however, will *on average* exceed the median by a magnitude greater than the magnitude by which the below-median values fall short of the median. Hence the expected value will exceed the median value.

Notes

1. I thank Alan Marcus for this intuition.

2. For a review of this assumption, see Chapter 4.

3. The normal deviate, in effect, rescales the distribution to have a mean of 0 and a standard deviation of 1. For a review of this topic, see Chapter 2.

4. Robert Ferguson deserves credit for the comment, "The expected value is not to be expected."

PART III

STRATEGY

17
Optimization

Optimization is a process by which we determine the most favorable tradeoff between competing interests, given the constraints we face. Within the context of portfolio management, the competing interests are risk reduction and return enhancement. Asset allocation is one form of optimization. We use an optimizer to identify the asset weights that produce the lowest level of risk for various levels of expected return. Optimization is also used to construct portfolios of securities that minimize risk in terms of tracking error relative to a benchmark portfolio. In these applications, we are usually faced with the constraint that the asset weights must sum to one.

We can also employ optimization techniques to manage strategies that call for offsetting long and short positions. Suppose, for example, that we wish to purchase currencies expected to yield high returns and to sell currencies expected to yield low returns, with the net result that we are neither long nor short the local currency. In this case, we would impose a constraint that the currency exposures sum to zero.

This chapter is intended as a tutorial on optimization. I will demonstrate, through the use of numerical examples, how to optimize a two-asset portfolio with only a pencil and the back of an envelope. If you wish to include three assets, you may need the front of the envelope as well. Beyond three assets, a computer would come in handy.

The Objective Function

Suppose we wish to identify the combinations of stocks and bonds that produce the lowest levels of risk for varying amounts of expected return. To begin, we must define a portfolio's expected return and risk.

The expected return of a portfolio comprised of just stocks and bonds is simply the weighted average of the assets' expected returns, as shown below:

$$R_p = (R_S \cdot W_S) + (R_B \cdot W_B) \tag{1}$$

where

R_p = the portfolio's expected return,

R_S = the expected return of stocks,

R_B = the expected return of bonds,

W_S = the percentage of the portfolio allocated to stocks and

W_B = the percentage allocated to bonds.

Portfolio risk is a little trickier. It is defined as volatility, and it is measured by the standard deviation or variance (the standard deviation squared) around the portfolio's expected return.[1] To compute a portfolio's variance, we must consider not only the variance of the component assets' returns, but also the extent to which the assets' returns co-vary.[2] The variance of a portfolio of stocks and bonds is computed as follows:

$$V = (\sigma_S^2 \cdot W_S^2) + (\sigma_B^2 \cdot W_B^2) + 2\rho(\sigma_S \cdot W_S)(\sigma_B \cdot W_B) \quad (2)$$

where

V = the portfolio variance,

σ_S = the standard deviation of stocks,

σ_B = the standard deviation of bonds and

ρ = the correlation between stocks and bonds.

Our objective, as stated earlier, is to minimize portfolio risk. Our first constraint is that the weighted average of the stock and bond returns must equal the expected return for the portfolio. We are also faced with a second constraint. We must allocate our entire portfolio to some combination of stocks and bonds. We would not want to leave part of it uninvested. Therefore, the fraction we allocate to stocks plus the fraction we allocate to bonds must equal one.

We can combine our objective and constraints to form the following objective function:

$$\Phi = [(\sigma_S^2 \cdot W_S^2) + (\sigma_B^2 \cdot W_B^2) + 2\rho(\sigma_S \cdot W_S)(\sigma_B \cdot W_B)]$$
$$+ [\lambda_1(R_S \cdot W_S + R_B \cdot W_B - R_p)] + [\lambda_2(W_S + W_B - 1)] \quad (3)$$

The first line of Equation (3) simply equals portfolio variance, the quantity to be minimized. The second line represents the two constraints. The first constraint ensures that the weighted average of the stock and bond returns equals the portfolio's expected return. The Greek letter lambda (λ) is called a Lagrange multiplier. It is a variable introduced to facilitate optimization when we face constraints, and it does not always lend itself to economic interpretation. The second constraint guarantees that the portfolio is fully invested. Again, lambda serves to facilitate a solution.

A Digression on Calculus

You may recall from elementary calculus that a function reaches its minimum or maximum value when its first derivative, or slope, equals zero. The first derivative measures the amount by which the value of the function changes given a one-unit change in the variable upon which it depends. Consider the following quadratic function:

$$y = x^2 - 4x + 10$$

If we set its derivative, $2x - 4$, equal to zero and solve for x, we find that this function reaches its minimum value when x equals 2. Figure 17.1 confirms this.

As Figure 17.1 shows, a function reaches its extreme value when it flattens out or has no slope, which is to say when its first derivative equals zero. With this insight, let us return to our objective function.

Unlike the quadratic function described above, which has a single unknown value, our objective function has four unknown values— the percentage of the portfolio to be allocated to stocks, the percentage to be allocated to bonds, the Lagrange multiplier for the first constraint and the Lagrange multiplier for the second constraint. To minimize portfolio risk given our constraints, we must take the par-

Figure 17.1   A Function

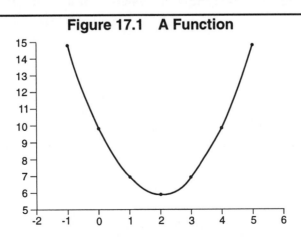

tial derivative of the objective function with respect to each asset weight and with respect to each Lagrange multiplier and set it equal to zero, as shown below:

$$\delta\Phi/\delta W_S = 2(\sigma_S{}^2 \cdot W_S) + 2\rho(\sigma_S \cdot \sigma_B \cdot W_{B)} + \lambda_1 \cdot R_S + \lambda_2 = 0 \quad (4)$$

$$\delta\Phi/\delta W_B = 2(\sigma_B{}^2 \cdot W_B) + 2\rho(\sigma_S \cdot W_S \cdot \sigma_B) + \lambda_1 \cdot R_B + \lambda_2 = 0 \quad (5)$$

$$\delta\Phi/\delta\lambda_1 = (R_S \cdot W_S) + (R_B \cdot W_B) - R_p = 0 \qquad (6)$$

$$\delta\Phi/\delta\lambda_2 = W_S + W_B - 1 = 0 \qquad (7)$$

Given assumptions for expected return, standard deviation and correlation (which I will identify later), we wish to find the values of W_S and W_B associated with different values of R_P, the portfolio's expected return. The values for λ_1 and λ_2 are merely mathematical byproducts of the solution.

One approach for solving a system of linear equations is by matrix inversion. Again, let us digress for a moment and focus on a simpler example of matrix inversion.[3]

A Digression on Matrix Algebra

In simple algebra, we would solve for x in an expression such as y = bx by dividing y by b. In matrix algebra, however, we cannot divide. The analogous operation is called matrix inversion.

Suppose we have the following system of linear equations:

$$6x_1 + 3x_2 + x_3 = 22$$

$$x_1 + 4x_2 - 2x_3 = 12$$

$$4x_1 - x_2 + 5x_3 = 10$$

We can represent this system of linear equations with a coefficient matrix, a vector for the variables and a vector for the constants, as follows:

$$\begin{bmatrix} 6 & 3 & 1 \\ 1 & 4 & -2 \\ 4 & -1 & 5 \end{bmatrix} \cdot \begin{bmatrix} x_1 \\ x_2 \\ x_3 \end{bmatrix} = \begin{bmatrix} 22 \\ 12 \\ 10 \end{bmatrix}$$

In order to solve for x_1, x_2 and x_3, we must find the inverse of the coefficient matrix and multiply it by the vector of constants. The inverse of the coefficient matrix is:[4]

$$\begin{bmatrix} 18/52 & -16/52 & -10/52 \\ -13/52 & 26/52 & 13/52 \\ -17/52 & 18/52 & 21/52 \end{bmatrix}$$

We multiply this inverse by the vector of constants to yield a vector with the values for x_1, x_2 and x_3, as follows

$$\begin{bmatrix} x_1 \\ x_2 \\ x_3 \end{bmatrix} = \begin{bmatrix} 18/52 & -16/52 & -10/52 \\ -13/52 & 26/52 & 13/52 \\ -17/52 & 18/52 & 21/52 \end{bmatrix} \cdot \begin{bmatrix} 22 \\ 12 \\ 10 \end{bmatrix} = \begin{bmatrix} 2 \\ 3 \\ 1 \end{bmatrix}$$

Now let us return to our system of linear equations and rewrite it in matrix notation.

$$\begin{bmatrix} 2 \cdot \sigma_S^2 & 2\rho\,(\sigma_S \cdot \sigma_B) & R_S & 1 \\ 2\rho\,(\sigma_S \cdot \sigma_B) & 2 \cdot \sigma_B{}^2 & R_B & 1 \\ R_S & R_B & 0 & 0 \\ 1 & 1 & 0 & 0 \end{bmatrix} \cdot \begin{bmatrix} W_S \\ W_B \\ \lambda_1 \\ \lambda_2 \end{bmatrix} = \begin{bmatrix} 0 \\ 0 \\ R_p \\ 1 \end{bmatrix}$$

We must next estimate the inputs for expected return, standard deviation and correlation. Suppose that, after careful examination of historical data and thorough analysis of current economic and capital market conditions, we arrive at the assumptions shown in Table 17.1.

With these assumptions, we can rewrite the coefficient matrix as follows:

$$\begin{bmatrix} 0.08 & 0.02 & 0.12 & 1.00 \\ 0.02 & 0.02 & 0.08 & 1.00 \\ 0.12 & 0.08 & 0.00 & 0.00 \\ 1.00 & 1.00 & 0.00 & 0.00 \end{bmatrix}$$

Table 17.1 Capital Market Assumptions

	Expected Return	Standard Deviation	Correlation
Stocks	12%	20%	
Bonds	8	10	50%

Its inverse equals:

$$\begin{bmatrix} 0 & 0 & 25 & -2 \\ 0 & 0 & -25 & 3 \\ 25 & -25 & -37.5 & 3 \\ -2 & 3 & 3 & -0.26 \end{bmatrix}$$

Because the constant vector includes a variable for the portfolio's expected return, we obtain a vector of formulas, rather than values, when we multiply the inverse matrix by the vector of constants, as shown below.

$$\begin{bmatrix} W_S \\ W_B \\ \lambda_1 \\ \lambda_2 \end{bmatrix} = \begin{bmatrix} 25 \cdot R_p - 2 \\ -25 \cdot R_p + 3 \\ -37.5 \cdot R_p + 3 \\ 3 \cdot R_p - 0.26 \end{bmatrix}$$

We are interested only in the first two formulas. The first formula yields the percentage to be invested in stocks in order to minimize risk when we substitute a value for the portfolio's expected return. The second formula yields the percentage to be invested in bonds. Table 17.2 shows the allocations to stocks and bonds that minimize risk for portfolio expected returns ranging from 8 percent to 13 percent.

From Table 17.2 we see that we must sell bonds short and leverage our exposure to stocks in order to achieve a portfolio expected return that is greater than the higher of the expected return on stocks or bonds.

Table 17.2 Optimal Portfolios

Expected Return	Standard Deviation	Stock %	Bond %
8.00%	10.00%	0	100
9.00	10.90	25	75
10.00	13.23	50	50
11.00	16.39	75	25
12.00	20.00	100	0
13.00	23.85	125	-25

An Alternative Approach

In 1987, William Sharpe published an algorithm for portfolio optimization that has the dual virtues of accommodating many real-world complexities while appealing to our intuition.[5] Consider the following objective function to be maximized.

$$\Phi = R - \lambda \cdot V \qquad (8)$$

where
R = portfolio expected return,
λ = a risk-aversion coefficient and
V = portfolio variance.

The risk-aversion coefficient measures how many units of expected return we are willing to sacrifice in order to reduce risk (variance) by one unit. By maximizing this objective function, we maximize expected return minus a quantity representing our aversion to risk times risk (as measured by variance).

Assume, again, that we have a portfolio consisting of stocks and bonds. Substituting the equations for portfolio expected return and variance (equations (1) and (2)), we can rewrite the objective function of equation (8) as follows:

$$(R_S \cdot W_S) + (R_B \cdot W_B) - \lambda[(\sigma_S{}^2 \cdot W_S{}^2)$$
$$+ (\sigma_B{}^2 \cdot W_B{}^2) + 2\rho(\sigma_S \cdot W_S \cdot \sigma_B \cdot W_B)] \qquad (9)$$

This objective function measures the expected utility or satisfaction we derive from a particular combination of expected return and risk, given our attitude toward risk. Its partial derivative with respect to each asset weight is:

$$\delta\Phi/\delta W_S = R_S - \lambda[2(\sigma_S^2 \cdot W_S) + 2\rho(\sigma_S \cdot W_B \cdot \sigma_B)] \qquad (10)$$

$$\delta\Phi/\delta W_B = R_B - \lambda[2(\sigma_B^2 \cdot W_B) + 2\rho(\sigma_S \cdot W_S \cdot \sigma_B)] \qquad (11)$$

The equation for each asset measures how much we can increase or decrease our expected utility, starting from our current asset mix, by increasing our exposure to that asset. A negative partial derivative indicates that we can improve expected utility by reducing exposure to that asset, while a positive partial derivative indicates that we should raise the exposure to that asset in order to improve our expected utility.

Let us retain our earlier assumptions about the expected returns and standard deviations of stocks and bonds and their correlation. Further, let us assume that our portfolio is currently allocated 60 percent to stocks and 40 percent to bonds and that our aversion toward risk equals 2. A risk-aversion coefficient of 2 means that we are willing to reduce expected return by two units in order to lower variance by one unit.

If we substitute these values into the partial derivative equations, we find that we can improve our expected utility by 0.008 units if we increase our exposure to stocks by 1 percent, and that we can improve our expected utility by 0.04 units if we increase our exposure to bonds by 1 percent. Both derivatives are positive. However, we can only allocate 100 percent of the portfolio. We should therefore increase our exposure to the asset class with the higher derivative by 1 percent and reduce by the same amount our exposure to the asset class with the lower derivative. In this way, we will ensure that we are always 100 percent invested.

Having switched our allocations in line with the relative magnitudes of the derivatives, we recompute the partial derivatives given our new allocation of 59 percent stocks and 41 percent bonds. Again, bonds have a higher derivative than stocks; hence we shift again from stocks to bonds. If we proceed in this fashion, we will find that when our portfolio is allocated ⅓ to stocks and ⅔ to bonds, the derivatives are exactly equal to each other. At this point, we cannot improve our expected utility any further by changing the allocation between stocks and bonds. We have maximized our objective function.

By varying the values we assign λ, we can identify mixes of stocks and bonds for many levels of risk-aversion, thus enabling us to construct the entire efficient frontier of stocks and bonds.

By now you are probably wondering why you should bother with fancy computer programs to optimize portfolios, since you can optimize them on the back of an envelope. I have purposely dealt with only two assets. As we increase the number of assets under consideration, we increase by a faster rate the number of variables to be included in our objective function. The sum of the number of expected returns, standard deviations and correlations to be included equals $(n^2 + n)/2$, where n equals the number of assets we wish to consider. Moreover, our examples are abstractions of real-world optimization problems. In the real world, we may be faced with short-selling constraints and other allocation constraints, as well as with transaction costs. Although it is certainly useful to understand the intuition and mathematical techniques that underlie optimization, most practical applications require sophisticated computer programs.

Error Maximization

There is a dark side to optimization, which we must not ignore. Cynics refer to it as "error maximization." In search of assets that increase a portfolio's expected return and lower its risk, optimization, by its vary nature, favors assets for which expected return is overestimated and risk underestimated.

Consider, for example, two assets, both of which have true mean returns of 10 percent. We do not know the true mean returns, however. We must estimate them, and in so doing we are vulnerable to errors. Suppose we estimate one asset to have a mean return of 8 percent and the other to have a mean return of 12 percent. If they both contribute the same degree of risk to the portfolio, the optimizer will favor the asset with the 12 percent return estimate.

This problem pertains as well to errors in our risk estimates. Moreover, the problem is exacerbated as we increase the number assets. The errors do not cancel each other out. Rather, they accumulate.

This bias leads to two problems. First, the expected return of the optimized portfolio is overstated, while its risk is understated. We can redress this problem to some extent by reducing our portfolio's estimated expected return or by augmenting its estimated risk to account for estimation error.

There is a more pernicious consequence of error maximization, though. Not only do we misestimate the portfolio's expected return and risk, we do so for the wrong portfolio. Essentially, we have excluded or underweighted assets for which we have underestimated return and overestimated risk, substituting for them assets for which we have erred in the opposite direction.

A common palliative for error maximization is to force the estimates to converge to their cross-sectional mean. We simply blend this mean with each individual estimate. For example, we might construct a new estimate for an asset's expected return by weighting the mean of all the expected return estimates by $\frac{1}{3}$ and the original estimate for that particular asset by $\frac{2}{3}$. This approach is limited, however, because it assumes that all our estimates are equally susceptible to error.

As an alternative, we might try to scale our estimates based on whatever information we can gather about their reliability. If we derive our estimates by extrapolating historical data, for example, we might wish to scale them as a function of the number of observations we used. At the very least, we should be sensitive to error maximization as we interpret our optimization results.

Notes

1. For a more detailed discussion of risk, see Chapter 2.

2. The notion of covariance is discussed in Chapter 1.

3. The inverse of a matrix is analogous to a reciprocal in simple algebra. If we multiply a matrix by its inverse, we get an identity matrix. An identity matrix includes ones along its diagonal and zeros for all the other elements. It is analogous to the number one in simple algebra, in that a matrix multiplied by an identity matrix yields itself. Multiplying a vector or matrix by the inverse of another matrix is analogous to multiplying a number by the reciprocal of another number; hence the analogy with division.

4. For a review of matrix operations, including multiplication and inversion, see A. Chaing, *Fundamental Methods of Mathematical Economics* (New York: McGraw-Hill, 1974), pp. 59–132.

5. W. Sharpe, "An Algorithm for Portfolio Improvement," *Advances in Mathematical Programming and Financial Planning, Vol. 1,* (Greenwich, CT: JAI Press Inç., 1987). Sharpe's algorithm can easily be adapted to accommodate transaction costs and allocation constraints.

18
Hedging

This chapter describes how to control risk through the use of financial futures and forward contracts. I begin with a discussion of the valuation of futures and forward contracts. Then I describe how they can be used to change the asset mix of a portfolio without disrupting the underlying assets. Next, I show how to hedge away the systematic risk and extract the alpha from an actively managed portfolio of short and long positions. I also describe how to remove the currency risk of an internationally diversified portfolio and demonstrate why full hedging is not necessarily optimal, even independent of any consideration about hedging costs. Finally, I show how to evaluate the tradeoff between the cost of hedging and risk reduction.[1]

Valuation of Financial Futures and Forward Contracts

A financial futures contract obligates a seller to pay the value of the futures contract to the buyer at a specified date. Financial futures contracts, which are marked to market daily, have uniform terms with respect to quantity, expiration date and underlying asset. Forward contracts, by contrast, are negotiated privately; their terms are thus specific to the transaction.

The fair value of a futures or forward contract is based on the notion of arbitrage. Suppose that the S&P 500 is valued at $450, that the three-month riskless interest rate is 1.50 percent, and that the S&P's expected dividend yield for the next three months equals 1.00 percent. The price of a futures contract on the S&P 500 that expires three months from now should equal $452.25. At this price, we are indifferent between purchasing the S&P 500 on margin or purchasing a futures contract on the index.

Assume that the value of a unit of an S&P 500 index fund equals 500 times the price of the index and that we purchase a unit with borrowed funds. Now suppose that, after three months, the S&P's price rises to $460, at which time we sell our unit. We receive $232,250—the price for which we sell our unit ($230,000) plus dividends equal to $2,250. At the same time, we must pay $228,375—the principal of our loan ($225,000) plus interest of $3,375, for a net gain of $3,875.

If we instead purchase a futures contract on the S&P 500 priced at $452.25 and sell it at expiration when its price equals $460, we earn the same profit—$3,875. The value of an S&P 500 futures contract equals the contract price times 500. We thus purchase the contract for $226,125 and sell it for $230,000.

What happens if the S&P 500 declines to $440 after three months? In this case, the strategy of purchasing the S&P 500 on margin loses $6,125. We experience a capital loss of $5,000, receive dividend income of $2,250, and incur an interest expense of $3,375. If we purchase a futures contract for $226,125 and sell it for $220,000, we experience the same loss of $6,125.

Table 18.1 illustrates the equivalence of a futures contract and a leveraged exposure to the underlying asset. In general, the value of a futures or forward contract equals the price of the underlying asset plus the cost of carry, which for financial assets is defined as the interest cost associated with purchasing the asset on margin less any income the asset generates during the term of the contract.

Table 18.1 Equivalence of Futures Contract and Leveraged Exposure

	S&P Leveraged	S&P Futures Contract
Purchase Price	225,000	226,125
	(450 x 500)	(452.25 x 500)
Interest Cost	3,375	0
	(0.015 x 225,000)	
Dividend Income	2,250	0
	(0.01 x 225,000)	
Sale Price	230,000	230,000
	(460 x 500)	(460 x 500)
Profit/Loss	3,875	3,875
Sale Price	220,000	220,000
	(440 x 500)	(440 x 500)
Profit/Loss	–6,125	–6,125

Arbitragers monitor the prices of futures contracts and their underlying assets and engage in arbitrage transactions whenever opportunities exist. This activity prevents futures prices from moving significantly away from their fair values. The range of values around fair value is determined by the ease with which arbitragers can profit from a misvalued futures contract. The more expensive or uncertain it is to transact in the underlying asset, the further away from fair value the futures price is likely to drift before arbitragers enter the market.

Asset Allocation with Futures Contracts

Suppose we have a $100 million portfolio, 60 percent of which is allocated to an S&P 500 index fund and 40 percent of which is allocated to a 20-year Treasury bond with a coupon yield of 8 percent. Also, suppose we wish to reduce its stock exposure to 40 percent and increase its bond exposure to 60 percent. One approach would be to sell the underlying S&P securities and invest the proceeds in Treasury bonds. Alternatively, we can sell S&P futures contracts and buy Treasury bond futures contracts as an overlay to our portfolio.

Because the value of an S&P 500 contract equals 500 times its price, we determine the number of contracts to sell as follows. We divide the value of the position we wish to trade ($20 million) by the quantity 500 times the S&P index price. At an S&P price of $450, we should sell 89 S&P futures contracts [20,000,000/(500 × 450)].[2]

Suppose that a 20-year Treasury bond with an 8 percent coupon is currently priced at $110-16/32. The value of a Treasury bond contract equals 1,000 times its price. We should therefore purchase 181 contracts in order to increase our bond exposure proportionately [20,000,000/(1,000 × 110.5)].

Now consider a situation in which we have a $100 million S&P 500 index fund, and we wish to convert 20 percent of it to Treasury bills. As was true in the previous example, we need to sell 89 S&P 500 futures contracts in order to reduce our stock exposure, but we need not purchase any Treasury bill futures contracts. Recall from the discussion about valuation that a futures contract is priced so that it is equivalent to purchasing the underlying asset on margin. The price of the contract equals the price of the underlying asset plus the implicit interest cost less the forgone dividend income. Therefore, by selling a futures contract against the underlying asset, we in effect create a Treasury bill exposure.

To see this equivalence, again suppose that the S&P 500 is valued at $450, that its dividend yield over the next three months equals 1.00 percent, and that the three-month riskless yield equals 1.50 percent. As shown earlier, a futures contract on the S&P 500 will be priced at $452.25.

Now suppose, as we did earlier, that the S&P price three months from now rises to $460 at which time the futures contract expires. The $20 million exposure to the S&P index yields dividend income equal to $200,000 and a capital gain of $444,444.44. At the same time, the 89 S&P futures contracts that were sold produce a capital loss of $344,875, for a net gain of $299,569.44, which is almost equivalent to a 1.5 percent yield. Had we been able to sell fractional contracts, this arbitrage would have generated precisely $300,000.

If the price of the S&P 500 falls to $440 three months hence, the $20 million exposure to the S&P index fund generates a capital loss of $444,444.44 and dividend income of $200,000. The short futures position produces a capital gain of $545,125, for a net gain of $300,680.56, which again equals a yield of about 1.5 percent.

Whether the S&P index rises or falls, a long position in the index together with an offsetting short exposure to S&P 500 futures contracts yields the riskless return, as long as the futures contracts are priced fairly. If they are priced below their fair value, this strategy will generate a return below the Treasury bill yield. If they are overpriced relative to their fair value, this strategy will generate a premium over the Treasury bill yield.

Now consider a situation in which we wish to change the allocation of a portfolio that consists of an actively managed equity component and an actively managed bond component. We do not wish to vitiate the value we expect to add through active management. We wish only to reallocate the assets so as to reduce our portfolio's exposure to the systematic risk of its equity component and to increase its exposure to the systematic risk of its bond component.

We measure the systematic risk of our equity portfolio by regressing its returns on the returns of the market, as represented by the S&P 500. The slope of the regression line is called beta, and it represents the sensitivity of our fund's return to the market's return. For example, if our fund's beta equals 1.2, and the S&P index returns 10 percent, we should expect our fund to return 12 percent. The extent to which its return is above or below 12 percent can be attributed to the active management of the fund.[3]

We compute the number of S&P contracts to sell in order to account for our equity portfolio's systematic risk as shown in equation (1):

$$N = A/S \times \beta \qquad (1)$$

where
   N = number of contracts to trade,
   A = amount to be reallocated,
   S = 500 times S&P 500 index price and
   β = beta of equity component.

If our equity component has a beta of 1.2 and we wish to reduce our portfolio's systematic equity risk 20 percent, we should sell 107 S&P 500 futures contracts. Although the value of these contracts is greater than $24 million, this transaction acts to lower our portfolio's systematic equity risk by only 20 percent while retaining its full exposure to security selection skill.

If we wish to increase our portfolio's bond exposure by 20 percent, we must determine the number of Treasury bond futures contracts that matches the systematic risk of our portfolio's bond component.

A bond's systematic risk is measured by its sensitivity to changes in the level of interest rates. This measure is called duration, and it equals the average time to receipt of a bond's cash flows weighted by its present values. If a bond's duration equals 10 and interest rates decline by one percentage point, the price of the bond will increase by 10 percent. Duration differs from term to maturity in two ways. First, term to maturity measures the time to receipt of the final principal repayment, whereas duration measures the average time remaining to receipt of all the cash flows, including coupon payments and interim principal repayments. Second, duration is weighted by the present values of the cash flows.[4]

If we wish to increase our portfolio's systematic bond risk by an amount equal to 20 percent of its value, we need to adjust the number of Treasury bond futures contracts that we acquire, as shown in equation (2):

$$N = A/S \times D_P/D_T \qquad (2)$$

where
  N = number of contracts,
  A = amount to be reallocated,
  S = 1,000 times underlying Treasury bond price,
  D_P = duration of portfolio bond component and
  D_T = duration of Treasury bond that underlies futures contract.

Suppose that the duration of the Treasury bond that underlies the futures contract equals 12, while the duration of our bond component equals 10. If, as assumed earlier, the value of a 20-year Treasury bond with an 8 percent coupon yield equals $110,500, we should purchase 151 contracts.[5] Although this transaction increases our bond exposure by only $16.61 million, it has the effect of creating a $20 million additional exposure to a bond with a duration equal to 10.

Short/Long Strategies

Suppose we wish to focus on stock selection and immunize our portfolio from broad market movements. That is, we wish to purchase stocks that we believe will outperform the market and to sell short stocks that we believe will underperform the market. If our long position and our short position have the same beta, we can eliminate systematic risk by purchasing and selling equal amounts. If, however, our long and short positions have different betas, then we must adjust our portfolio's long and short exposures to account for the difference in their betas if we want to eliminate systematic risk.

Suppose, for example, that our long position has a beta equal to 1.0 while the beta of our short position equals 0.9. There are various ways we can eliminate systematic risk. For example, we can limit our long position to 90 percent of our short position. This approach, however, places more emphasis on our ability to identify stocks with negative alphas than to identify stocks with positive alphas. As an alternative, we can establish equal long and short exposures to the individual stocks and sell S&P 500 futures contracts to offset 10 percent of our long position. This approach reduces the systematic risk of our long position to that of our short position, while maintaining equal exposure to the stock-specific risk of our long and short positions.

If we believe that our stock selection skill is limited to identifying stocks that we expect to outperform the S&P 500, we can neutralize our market exposure by selling S&P futures contracts in an amount based upon the beta of our long position. If we feel more comfortable identifying stocks that we expect to underperform the market, we can eliminate our fund's market exposure by purchasing S&P contracts in an amount based upon the beta of our short position.

Hedging Currency Exposure

The notion of beta can also be applied to hedging currency exposure. Suppose we allocate a fraction of our portfolio to overseas investments. How much of the embedded currency risk of these investments should we hedge? One approach is to sell currency forward or futures contracts in an amount equal to the currency exposure of our investments. Typically, however, this approach will not minimize the currency risk of our portfolio. We are more likely to reduce currency risk if we condition the amount we hedge on the beta of our portfolio with respect to the relevant currency.

Suppose that 30 percent of our portfolio is allocated to the Japanese stock market. Assume that our portfolio has a standard deviation of 12 percent, that the yen has a standard deviation of 10 percent, that our portfolio is 15 percent correlated with the yen, and that independent of any change in the value of the yen, our portfolio has an expected return of 10 percent. We can think of this independent return as our portfolio's alpha with respect to movements in the yen. In order to minimize the volatility of our portfolio's return that is associated with changes in the dollar/yen exchange rate, we should sell a forward contract on the yen in amount equal to 18 percent of our portfolio's value; which is to say, we should hedge 60 percent of our portfolio's yen exposure.

The reason that we should hedge only 60 percent of our currency exposure in order to minimize risk is that our portfolio's beta with respect to the yen is 18 percent, and 18 percent of our 30 percent yen exposure equals 60 percent.

A portfolio's beta with respect to the yen equals its correlation with the yen times its standard deviation divided by the yen's standard deviation, as equation (3) shows:

$$\beta = \rho \times \sigma_p / \sigma_c \qquad (3)$$

where
β = portfolio beta with respect to currency,
ρ = correlation between portfolio and currency,
σ_p = portfolio standard deviation and
σ_c = currency standard deviation.

In order to determine the effectiveness of this currency hedging strategy, let us assume that the yen and the yen forward contract will either increase or decrease by 10 percent. If it increases 10 percent and we do not hedge any of the portfolio's currency exposure, we should expect the portfolio to return 11.8 percent—the sum of the 10 percent expected return that is independent of the yen's return plus 0.18 times the yen's return. By the same reasoning, we should expect the portfolio to return 8.2 percent should the yen decline by 10 percent.

Now suppose we hedge all the portfolio's exposure to the yen; that is, we sell a forward contract on the yen equal to 30 percent of the portfolio's value. If the yen increases by 10 percent, we should expect the portfolio to return 8.8 percent—the sum of the underlying portfolio's return plus the return of the short forward position (-3.0 percent). If the yen falls by 10 percent, we add the 3 percent return from the short forward position to the return of the underlying portfolio; our expected return is now 11.2 percent.

If instead we sell short a forward contract on the yen in an amount equal to 18 percent of our portfolio, which equals 60 percent of our yen exposure, we should expect to eliminate fully the portfolio risk that arises from uncertainty in the yen exchange rate. If the yen rises 10 percent, the forward position loses 1.8 percent for a net return of 10.0 percent. If the yen falls 10 percent, we gain 1.8 percent on the short forward position, which when added to the underlying portfolio's return again equals 10 percent. Table 18.2 summarizes these results.

We can also verify that a beta-derived currency hedge ratio minimizes portfolio risk by computing the standard deviation of a portfolio combined with a short position in a currency forward contract, as shown in equation (4):

$$\sigma_{P+F} = (\sigma_P^2 + \sigma_F^2 \times W^2 + 2 \times \rho \times \sigma_P \times \sigma_F \times W)^{1/2} \qquad (4)$$

Table 18.2 Effectiveness of Alternative Currency Hedging Strategies

Portfolio Beta with Respect to Yen: 18%
Portfolio Alpha with Respect to Yen: 10%
Portfolio Exposure to Yen: 30%

Alpha +	Beta ×	Yen Return +	Forward Exposure ×	Yen Return =	Portfolio Return
			Unhedged		
10%	18%	10%	0%	10%	11.8%
10	18	−10	0	−10	8.2
			Fully Hedged		
10%	18%	10%	−30%	10%	8.8%
10	18	−10	−30	−10	11.2
			Optimally Hedged		
10%	18%	10%	−18%	10%	10.0%
10	18	−10	−18	−10	10.0

where

σ_{P+F} = standard deviation of combination of portfolio
and forward contract,

σ_P = standard deviation of underlying portfolio,

σ_F = standard deviation of currency forward contract,

W = weighting of currency forward contract, and

ρ = correlation of underlying portfolio
and currency forward contract.

By substituting the assumptions given earlier into equation (4), we find that the standard deviation of the fully hedged strategy equals 11.92 percent, versus 11.86 percent for the beta-derived hedging strategy. Although this difference may seem rather small, to the extent we incur transaction costs to hedge currency exposure, the beta-derived hedging strategy is less expensive to implement as long as the beta is less than our portfolio's currency exposure.

Risk Reduction versus Cost of Hedging

In the currency hedging example, I assumed that we wish to minimize portfolio risk as a function of currency exposure regardless of the expected cost of hedging. It is more likely that we would seek to balance risk reduction with the cost of hedging.

The cost of hedging currency risk has several components. There are transaction costs as well as management and administrative fees. In addition, the currency futures or forward contract will sell at discount to the spot exchange rate when domestic interest rates are lower than foreign interest rates. If the spot exchange rate does not decline to the current forward rate, we will incur a loss on our short forward position. The opposite may also be true; we might experience a gain if we sell a currency forward contract at a premium and the spot rate fails to appreciate to the forward rate prevailing at the time we sell the contract.

In any event, to the extent we have reason to believe that a currency forward contract's expected return is different from zero, we should reflect this view in our estimate of the cost of hedging. If we anticipate a positive return, we should raise our estimate of the hedging cost by this amount. If we expect a negative return, we should lower our cost estimate.

Once we estimate the cost of hedging, we need to determine how many units of cost we are willing to incur at the margin in order to lower our portfolio's variance by one unit. We can infer this tradeoff from our choice of the underlying portfolio. It is the slope of a line that is tangent to the efficient frontier at the location of our portfolio's expected return and risk, assuming risk is measured in units of variance.

The exposure to a currency forward contract that optimally balances our aversion to risk with our reluctance to incur costs is given by equation (5), assuming our portfolio is exposed to only one foreign currency.[6] This equation is derived by taking the partial derivative of expected utility with respect to exposure to the currency forward contract and setting this value equal to zero.

$$W = C/(2 \times \lambda \times \sigma_F^2) - \rho \times \sigma_P/\sigma_F \qquad (5)$$

where
    W = optimal exposure to currency forward contract
          as a fraction of portfolio value,
    C = expected cost of hedging, including expected return
          of forward contract,
    λ = tradeoff between risk reduction and cost,

σ_F = standard deviation of currency forward contract,

σ_P = standard deviation of underlying portfolio, and

ρ = correlation of currency forward contract
and underlying portfolio.

Suppose, for example, we estimate hedging costs to equal 0.25 percent and we determine that we are willing to incur two units of incremental cost to reduce our portfolio's variance by one unit. Based on our earlier assumptions about correlation and standard deviations, we should sell a forward contract on the yen equal to 11.75 percent of our portfolio's value, which corresponds to 39.17 percent of its exposure to the yen. Although this hedging strategy does not minimize the risk due to currency exposure, it optimally balances our willingness to incur cost in order to lower risk.

I have attempted to present some of the basic principles of hedging with financial futures and forward contracts. I have ignored much of the administrative detail associated with the application of these principles. Those who are interested in these important details should consult other sources, including those referenced in the notes.

Notes

1. Those who are interested in a more detailed review of these topics should see S. Figlewski in collaboration with K. John and J. Merrick, *Hedging with Financial Futures for Institutional Investors: From Theory to Practice* (Cambridge, MA: Ballinger Publishing Company, 1986).

2. This result ignores the fact that financial futures contracts are marked to market daily. As a consequence, gains and losses accrue in an interest-bearing margin account. In order to adjust for this daily mark-to-market feature, we should reduce the hedge position to its present value. This adjustment is called "tailing the hedge."

3. According to the Capital Asset Pricing Model, we should estimate systematic risk by regressing a portfolio's returns in excess of the riskless return on the market's excess returns. To the extent the riskless return is stable, though, this approach will yield a similar estimate.

4.   For a more detailed description of duration, see Chapter 6.

5.   Treasury bond futures contracts can be settled by delivery of a variety of bonds. Therefore, it is sometimes necessary to adjust the hedge ratio by a delivery factor that equates a deliverable bond to the reference bond.

6.   This framework assumes that we only sell currency forward contracts. If we were to consider purchasing forward contracts, we would reflect the hedging cost net of a forward contract's expected return as a negative value.

19
Option Replication

A financial option gives the owner the right to buy (in the case of a call option) or to sell (in the case of a put option) an asset at a specified price. This right, in the case of an American option, can be exercised at any time over a specified period. (A European option can be exercised only at a specific date.) Exchange-traded options are available on a large variety of individual securities, as well as on stock indexes and foreign currencies.

Despite the wide availability of exchange-traded options, the demand for option-like payoffs vastly exceeds the supply. A large market in privately negotiated options and in option-replication strategies has emerged. This generates option-like results for assets or portfolios on which exchange-traded options are not available or for terms different from the typical terms of exchange-traded options. This column demonstrates how we can generate an option-like payoff by shifting a fund between two assets.

Hedging Currency Risk

Suppose a corporation based in London expects to receive 75 million deutschemarks one year from today. The CFO is concerned that the mark might depreciate relative to the pound during this period. Let us assume that the spot exchange rate currently equals three marks per pound, so that the receivable is worth 25 million pounds today. What are the CFO's alternatives for hedging this risk?

One approach is to sell 75 million marks forward. Under this strategy, if the mark depreciates, as feared by the CFO, the loss that will occur when the 75 million marks are converted into pounds will be offset exactly by the gain on the forward contract. That is the good news. The bad news is that any gain, should the mark instead *appreciate* relative to the pound, will be offset by an equivalent loss on the forward contract.

Ideally, the CFO would like to protect the firm's receipts against a possible decline in the mark relative to the pound and to profit in the event the mark appreciates. An option to exchange 75 million marks for 25 million pounds one year from now would achieve these contingent results. If the mark depreciates, the CFO collects the 75 million marks and, under the terms of the option contract, exchanges them for 25 million pounds regardless of the prevailing exchange rate. Alternatively, if the mark appreciates, the option expires worthless, but the CFO exchanges the marks for pounds at the higher exchange rate.

Of course, this privilege is not without cost. The CFO must pay a premium for the option to exchange marks for pounds at today's exchange rate. She will suffer a net loss if the mark depreciates or fails to appreciate sufficiently to offset the option premium. Her maximum loss is limited to the amount of the option premium (assuming the exercise price is based on the current exchange rate), while her potential gain is unlimited. Therefore, let us suppose that she chooses to pursue the option strategy.

How should she proceed? There are no exchange-traded options to convert marks to pounds one year forward, nor can such options be constructed by combining exchange-traded options to exchange pounds for dollars and dollars for marks. But many financial institutions, including large brokerage firms and banks, offer privately negotiated options to meet specific customer requirements. These institutions are motivated by the fact that they can usually hedge the risk exposure incurred by writing the option at a lower cost than the premium they charge.

Option Replication Using the Binomial Model

Under perfect market conditions, one can replicate the contingent payoff of an option by shifting funds between a riskless asset (in our example, the one-year Treasury bill in the United Kingdom) and a risky asset (the mark). In order to demonstrate this correspondence, let us begin by making the simplifying assumption that the mark, which we assumed earlier can be exchanged for 0.3333 pounds today, will either increase 10 percent or decrease 10 percent one year hence, and that these outcomes are equally probable. Moreover, in order to focus the discussion on the essence of option replication, we will make the convenient but obviously false assumption that the riskless rate of interest is 6 percent in the United Kingdom and 0 percent in Germany. Thus the only possible values for the receivable of

75 million marks, which today can be exchanged for 25 million pounds, are 27.5 million pounds (mark appreciates 10 percent) and 22.5 million pounds (mark depreciates 10 percent), as Figure 19.1 shows.

We can easily determine the value of an option to exchange 75 million marks for 25 million pounds one year hence. The option will be worth nothing if the mark appreciates to 0.3667, because at this value 75 million marks can be exchanged for 27.5 million pounds. If the mark falls in value to 0.3000, however, the option will be worth 2.5 million pounds—the difference between the 25 million pounds for which the marks could be exchanged under the terms of the option contract and 22.5 million pounds, which is the pound-equivalent of 75 million marks at an exchange rate of 0.3000. These contingent values are shown in parentheses in Figure 19.1.

Given the obvious values for an option to exchange marks for pounds one year from now, we can construct two equations that, when solved simultaneously, reveal how we can hedge the option by combining exposure to the mark and a riskless asset:

$$27,500,000 \cdot M + 1.06 \cdot P = 0$$

$$22,500,000 \cdot M + 1.06 \cdot P = 2,500,000$$

Here, M represents exposure to the mark, while P represents exposure to the U.K. Treasury bill, both from the perspective of our British CFO. Recall our earlier assumptions that the riskless return is 6 percent in the U.K. and 0 percent in Germany. By solving these equations simultaneously, we find that M equals -0.5000 and P equals 12,971,698. This indicates that we can hedge an option to exchange 75 million marks for 25 million pounds one year from now by selling marks short in an amount equal to 12.5 million pounds and investing 12,971,698 pounds at 6 percent, the riskless rate of interest in the U.K.

Figure 19.1   Binomial Model

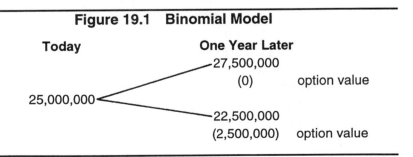

Today	One Year Later
	27,500,000
	(0) option value
25,000,000	
	22,500,000
	(2,500,000) option value

Furthermore, the "fair value" of this option today must equal the sum of our short position in the mark and our long position in the U.K. Treasury bill, which equals 471,698 pounds.

To validate the equivalence between this hedging strategy and an option to exchange 75 million marks for 25 million pounds one year forward, let us consider the payoff to the institution that writes the option and then hedges it as we just described, assuming it charges the aforementioned fair value of 471,698 pounds as the premium. If the mark rises 10 percent, the option will expire worthless. At the same time, the short position in the mark will produce a loss of 1,250,000 pounds, while the long position in the Treasury bill will yield a gain of 778,302 pounds for a net loss to the hedging strategy of 471,698 pounds. This loss exactly offsets the premium received for writing the option.

If the mark declines 10 percent, the option will be worth 2 million pounds. Thus the net loss for writing the option will equal 2,028,302 pounds. The short position in the mark, however, will yield a profit of 1,250,000 pounds, which when combined with the yield from the investment in the Treasury bill of 778,302 pounds totals 2,028,302 pounds. This exactly offsets the net loss from writing the option. Table 19.1 summarizes these results.

Table 19.1 Option Payoffs

Mark Rises 10 Percent:

Put Value:	0
Premium Received:	471,698
Net Return from Writing Option:	471,698
Mark Payoff (−12,500,000 · 0.1):	−1,250,000
Treasury Bill Payoff (12,971,698 · 0.06):	778,302
Net Return from Hedging Strategy:	−471,698

Mark Falls 10 Percent:

Put Value (25,000,000 − 22,500,000):	2,500,000
Premium Received:	471,698
Net Return from Writing Option:	−2,028,302
Mark Payoff (−12,500,000 · −0.1):	1,250,000
Treasury Bill Payoff (12,971,698 · 0.06):	778,302
Net Return from Hedging Strategy:	2,028,302

From the payoffs described in this example, it easy to see that the institution writing the option can earn a riskless profit as long as it charges a premium in excess of 471,698 pounds. These results, however, depend on the simplifying assumption that the mark can only increase or decrease by 10 percent in the course of a year, and that both outcomes are equally likely. This assumption is, of course, false. The exchange rate between the pound and the mark changes continually throughout the day, every business day. The basic methodology described above can, however, be expanded to accommodate real-world conditions. Expanding the binomial tree in Figure 19.1 to include small changes in the value of the mark over many short time intervals, based on a realistic estimate of the mark's volatility, would allow us to derive a more precise estimate of the option's fair value today and as the year unfolds. In order to hedge this option, we would need to revise the exposure to the mark and the Treasury bill continually as the mark's value changes and as time passes.

Option Replication Using the Continuous-Time Black-Scholes Model

As the discrete time intervals in the binomial tree become smaller, approaching zero, the results of the binomial model resemble the results that would be obtained by using a variation of the continuous-time Black-Scholes model.

Based on the insights of the Black-Scholes model, we can determine the value of an option to exchange marks for a fixed amount of pounds from a British investor's perspective by using the following formula:

$$P = Xe^{-r_d T} \cdot N[-(D - \sigma\sqrt{T})] - Me^{-r_f T} \cdot N[-D]$$

where

P = value of option

M = value of mark denominated in pounds,

X = strike price,

T = time remaining until expiration,

r_d = instantaneous riskless rate of interest in U.K. $\ln(1 + r)$,

r_f = instantaneous riskless rate of interest in Germany $\ln(1 + r)$,

$D = [\ln(M/X) + (r_d - r_f + \sigma^2/2) \cdot T]/(\sigma\sqrt{T})$,

$\ln( )$ = natural log,

σ = standard deviation of the return on the mark and

N( ) = cumulative normal distribution function.

Let us relax our earlier assumption that Germany's riskless interest rate is 0 percent. If the foreign riskless rate were 0 percent, the formula would converge exactly to the Black-Scholes formula for a non-dividend-paying stock. Within the context of a currency option, the interest payment can be thought of as a dividend on the currency so that the formula for valuing a currency option is analogous to the formula used to value a European option on a dividend-paying stock.

In order to illustrate the application of this formula to hedge an option to exchange marks for a fixed amount of pounds, let us retain our earlier assumptions and make the additional assumptions that Germany's riskless rate equals 5 percent and the mark's standard deviation equals 10 percent. These assumptions are shown below:

M = 25 million pounds,
X = 25 million pounds,
T = one year,
r_d = ln(1.06) = 5.83 percent,
r_f = ln(1.05) = 4.88 percent and
σ = 10 percent.

By substituting these values into the above formula, we discover that the currency option's fair value equals 836,918 pounds. The hedge ratio equals –0.421. This value determines the exposure to the mark, which, when combined with investment in the Treasury bill, hedges the option. To hedge an option to exchange 75 million marks for 25 million pounds, we must thus start out by selling marks short in an amount equivalent to 10,534,272 pounds. By netting this short position out of our original exposure of 25 million pounds and adding to it the value of the option, we discover the amount to invest in U.K. Treasury bills, which equals 15,302,645 pounds.

The exposures derived above represent the starting positions to hedge the option. As the exchange rate between the mark and the pound changes, and as time passes, we must repeat the exercise to determine the current exposures; this explains the term *dynamic hedging*. As long as the mark's exchange rate does not change so abruptly that we cannot execute the requisite trades and as long as transaction costs are not a factor, this dynamic hedging strategy should effectively hedge an option to exchange 75 million marks for 25 million pounds one year from now.

Because the institution that writes the option is contractually obligated to deliver 25 million pounds in exchange for 75 million marks should the mark's value decline, it bears the risk that its hedging strategy may not perform as expected. As compensation for bearing this risk, and to cover transaction costs, the institution will charge a higher premium than the theoretical premium implied by the option pricing formula. If the spread between the actual premium and the theoretically fair premium is judged to be unreasonably wide, the customer always has the option to self-insure by implementing the dynamic hedging strategy internally.

20
Commodity Futures Contracts

During the past decade, institutional investors have sought to diversify their portfolios by investing in less traditional assets such as foreign securities, real estate and venture capital. More recently, some institutions have considered commodities as a potential investment. Historically, commodities have had a negative correlation with traditional asset classes and have offered an effective hedge against inflation.

This chapter reviews the market and describes the sources of value for nonfinancial commodity futures contracts. These contracts fall into four broad categories—grains and oil seeds, livestock and meat, food and fiber, and metals and petroleum.[1]

Commodity Futures Markets

A commodity futures contract obligates the seller to deliver a particular quantity and grade of a commodity to the buyer at a predetermined date and location, for a price agreed upon at the time of the transaction. The terms of the contract are standardized. Only the price of the contract changes with the passage of time. This standardization distinguishes futures contracts from forward contracts, the terms of which must be negotiated privately between the buyer and the seller for each contract. Unlike forward contracts, futures contracts also require margin deposits and are marked to market daily.

Although a commodity futures contract calls for delivery of the relevant commodity at the time of settlement, most futures contracts are liquidated by executing an offsetting transaction prior to the settlement date. If a trader is long July 10, 1993 cotton contracts, he simply enters an order to sell July 10, 1993 cotton contracts in order to close his position. If he were short the contracts, he would liquidate his position by entering an order to buy July 10, 1993 cotton contracts.

If a trader with a long position in commodity futures contracts neglects to liquidate his position by executing an offsetting transaction, he takes delivery of the physical commodity (unless the contract calls for cash settlement). Delivery does not mean that a trader might arrive home one evening from a stressful day at the office only to find live hogs collectively weighing in at 400,000 pounds roaming around his finely manicured suburban lawn. Each contract designates a location with suitable facilities for delivery. The trader might, however, be required to pay storage and insurance costs while he seeks a buyer for his hogs.

Many commodity futures contracts are entered into by suppliers and consumers of the commodity desiring to hedge their existing exposure. Consequently, some contracts are liquidated by a transaction called an exchange of futures for physicals. For example, a wheat farmer who has yet to harvest his crop may have sold wheat futures contracts to protect himself from a potential decline in the price of wheat. In the meantime, a miller may have purchased wheat futures contracts as a hedge against a price increase prior to the time he is ready to buy the wheat. These parties might agree to exchange wheat for their futures contracts, assuming the wheat can be harvested and delivered before the settlement date of the contract.

Some commodity futures contracts specify cash settlement. For these contracts, the gain or loss that results when the futures price converges to the spot price at the settlement date is simply transferred to the appropriate party.

Commodity futures contracts are traded by institutions called futures commission merchants. A futures commission merchant (FCM) essentially performs the same function as a brokerage house. It maintains trading accounts for its customers, executes trades at the exchanges, and collects margin deposits from its customers.

There are numerous exchanges in the United States and around the world on which commodity futures contracts are traded. They include the Chicago Board of Trade, the Chicago Mercantile Exchange and the New York Mercantile Exchange. In 1990, nearly 110 million nonfinancial commodity futures contracts were traded in the United States. More than 70 percent of these trades occurred on the three exchanges mentioned above.[2]

Exchanges, which are sometimes referred to as contract markets, set margin requirements for each contract. When a trader purchases a futures contract, he is not required to pay the value of the contract to the FCM at that time. Instead, he must deposit initial margin in the form of a Treasury bill or a bank letter of credit. The initial margin is, in effect, a performance bond, and the amount required varies from contract to contract, typically as a function of the volatility of the underlying commodity. The amount also depends on whether the trader is hedging an existing exposure to the underlying commodity or simply speculating in the commodity. The initial margin requirement is usually greater for speculators than it is for hedgers.

Once a trader establishes a position in a futures contract, he is also required to pay daily variation margin to cover trading losses as they occur. Suppose, for example, that a trader is long 10 contracts that, as of the previous close, were valued at $50,000 each. Now suppose that at the close of today's trading these contracts settle at a price of $49,500. The total position falls in value by $5,000. The trader must therefore transfer $5,000 from his account to the account of the FCM to cover this loss. If the contracts rise in value to $51,000 the next day, the FCM must transfer $15,000 to the trader's account to meet the required variation margin. Thus the gains and losses of futures contracts are settled on a daily basis, even though the position remains open.

Each exchange is affiliated with a clearinghouse that performs two functions. First, it provides a mechanism by which exchange members clear their positions. Second, it ensures the financial integrity of the exchange by monitoring the credit-worthiness of exchange members and by maintaining capital funds as protection against the potential insolvency of any of the members.

Trades are cleared through the following mechanism. The members of the exchange report all their trades to the associated clearinghouse. Once the clearinghouse accepts these trades, it replaces the exchange members as the buyers and the sellers of the contracts. It matches all the trades and computes the members' net gains and losses. The clearinghouse then collects the appropriate payments from the members with net losses and disburses them to the members with net gains.

The federal regulatory agency that oversees trading in commodity futures contracts is called the Commodity Futures Trading Commission (CFTC). It was established in 1974 and derives its authority from the Commodity Exchange Act. The CFTC fulfills a role that is analogous to the function of the Securities and Exchange Commission. Essentially, it is responsible for promoting fair and efficient pricing, trading integrity and financial soundness.

Reporting on Commodity Trading

Below, I review an example of the type of information about commodity futures contracts that is reported in the financial press. The December 17, 1992 edition of *The Wall Street Journal* reported the information given in Table 20.1 for futures contracts on soybean meal. CBT refers to the Chicago Board of Trade, the exchange where futures contracts on soybean meal are traded. Each contract represents 100 tons of soybean meal, and the quoted prices are the dollars per ton for the contracts.

On December 16, 1992, the contract for May 1993 delivery opened at $184 per ton for a total price of $18,400, which was also its high for the day. It traded as low as $183.10 and settled for the day at $183.70, which was $0.70 below the prior day's closing price. The lifetime high for the May 1993 contract was $210, and its lifetime low was $179.40. As of the close of trading on December 16, 1992, 12,172 contracts remained open. This figure refers to either the long positions or the short positions, not to the sum of the long and short positions, because each long position is also a short position.

The estimated volume on Wednesday, December 16, 1992, was 16,000 contracts, compared with 14,719 contracts on the previous Tuesday. The open interest for all the soybean meal contracts traded on the Chicago Board of Trade totaled 73,780 contracts, a reduction of 1,175 contracts from the previous day.

Note the prices of the various contracts. The prices of the December 1992 through May 1993 contracts decrease with the time remaining to settlement. Beginning with the July 1993 contract, however, the prices of the contracts start to increase with further increases in the time remaining to settlement. The next section reviews the valuation of commodity futures contracts and explains why prices vary as a function of the time remaining to the settlement date.

Valuing Commodity Futures Contracts

The fair value of a commodity futures contract is based on the principle of arbitrage. Suppose we purchase 100 troy ounces of gold at $350 per ounce and finance this purchase by borrowing $35,000 at a total cost of $500 for three months. Suppose, at the end of three months, the price of a troy ounce of gold appreciates to $365, at

Table 20.1 Trading Activity for Futures Contracts on Soybean Meal

	Open	High	Low	Settle	Change	Lifetime High	Lifetime Low	Open Interest
Soybean Meal (CBT) 100 tons: $ per ton								
Dec	188.30	188.30	187.40	188.20	-0.50	209.00	176.50	3,013
Ja93	185.70	185.70	184.50	185.60	-0.20	209.00	177.40	21,934
Mar	184.70	184.50	183.40	184.00	-0.60	210.00	178.30	23,230
May	184.00	184.00	183.10	183.70	-0.70	210.00	179.40	12,172
July	185.10	185.20	184.30	184.80	-0.70	208.00	181.30	9,840
Aug	185.70	186.00	185.20	185.50	-0.40	193.50	182.20	1,751
Sept	186.50	186.70	186.20	186.40	-0.50	193.50	183.10	1,217
Oct	188.00	188.00	187.50	188.00	-0.70	194.50	185.50	416
Dec	189.00	189.00	189.00	189.00	-1.00	191.50	187.20	207

Est vol 16,000: vol Tues 14,719; open int 73,780; 1,175

Source: *The Wall Street Journal,* December 17, 1992.

which time we sell the 100 ounces and repay the loan. Our total profit from these transactions equals $1,000 ($36,500 – $35,000 – $500).

Now suppose that, instead of purchasing 100 ounces of gold on margin, we purchase a futures contract for 100 ounces of gold for settlement in three months. The fair value of this contract equals the price that yields a $1,000 profit if we hold this futures contract until the settlement date, when it will be worth $36,500. A purchase price of $35,500 yields a profit of $1,000 under this scenario.[3]

If the futures contract sells for less than $35,500—say $35,200—we could sell 100 ounces of gold short and lend the proceeds of $35,000, earning interest income of $500. At the same time, we could purchase the futures contract at a price of $35,200 and hold it until the settlement date. By then we will have earned a profit of $1,300 on the futures transaction, experienced a loss of $1,500 on the short sale, and earned interest income of $500 for a net profit of $300 without any capital outlay or risk exposure.

If the futures contract sells for $36,000, we could sell the futures contract and borrow $35,000 to purchase 100 ounces of gold. By the settlement date, we will have earned a $1,500 profit on our long position in the gold, suffered a loss of $500 on our short futures position, and incurred an interest expense of $500 for a net profit of $500, again without any capital outlay or exposure to risk.

Arbitragers monitor the prices of futures contracts and their underlying commodities and engage in arbitrage transactions whenever the opportunity arises. This activity prevents futures prices from deviating significantly from their fair values.

The pricing model used to determine the fair value of a commodity futures contract is called the cost-of-carry model. According to this model, the fair value of a commodity futures contract equals the spot price of the underlying commodity plus the cost of carrying the commodity, which in the previous example is the financing cost. If we assume that the cost of carrying the commodity is comprised entirely of the financing cost, the cost-of-carry model supposes that the profit or loss on a long futures position equals the profit or loss from acquiring the underlying commodity on margin. Table 20.2 summarizes this relationship.

Thus far we have assumed that the cost of carry is comprised only of the financing cost of acquiring the commodity on margin. Although the financing cost accounts for the preponderance of the cost

**Table 20.2 Equivalence of Futures Position
and Leveraged Acquisition**

	Underlying Commodity	Futures Contract
Beginning Price:	$350	$355
Financing Cost:	5	0
Spot Price Appreciates to:	365	365
Net Profit:	10	10
Spot Price Depreciates to:	340	340
Net Loss:	−15	−15

of carry for precious metals, a significant component of the cost of carrying other commodities consists of storage and transportation costs; for commodities for which the risk of spoilage or damage is a consideration, insurance costs can be significant. If we take all these costs into account, the fair value of a commodity futures contract equals the spot price of the underlying commodity plus the financing, insurance, storage and transportation costs.

Because the collective costs of carrying a commodity are positive, we might expect the price of a futures contract to exceed the spot price of the underlying commodity. Moreover, as the settlement date approaches, we might expect the difference between the price of the underlying commodity and the price of the futures contract to diminish, because the cost of carrying the commodity diminishes with the passage of time. The difference between the spot price and the futures price is called the basis. If the futures price exceeds the spot price, the relationship is referred to as *contango*.

Table 20.1 reveals that the prices of some of the longer-dated contracts are lower than the prices of some of the shorter-dated contracts. For example, the May 1993 contract settled at $183.70 per ton compared with $185.60 for the January 1993 contract. What's more, the spot price for soybean meal as of the close of trading on December 16, 1992, was $189 per ton based on the average of the bid-ask spread reported in *The Wall Street Journal* the next day.[4] This relationship seems to imply that the cost of carrying soybean meal is negative, a rather unlikely proposition.

When the spot price of the commodity exceeds the price of the futures contract, the futures contract is said to be in *backwardation*.

Based on the arbitrage concept described earlier, backwardation would appear to offer a free lunch.

In theory, an owner of soybean meal could sell his supply at $18,900 per 100 tons, lend the proceeds of this sale at the available five-month interest rate of 1.4 percent, and thereby earn interest of $264.60. At the same time, he could purchase a May 1993 futures contract on soybean meal for $18,370. These transactions would guarantee a riskless profit of $794.60 per 100 tons of soybean meal relative to holding the current supply of soybean meal.[5]

To validate this result, suppose the price of soybean meal appreciates to $195 per ton. The futures position yields a gain of $1,130.00 per contract, which, together with the interest proceeds of $264.60, results in a total gain of $1,394.60. This gain exceeds by $794.60 the forgone profit of $600 per 100 tons of soybean meal the owner would have realized had he kept his supply of soybean meal.

If, instead, the price of soybean meal declines to $185 per ton, the futures position produces a gain of $130 per contract, which is increased by interest proceeds of $264.60 per 100 tons. Had he kept his supply of soybean meal, the owner would have lost $400 per 100 tons. Thus his net advantage again equals $794.60.

To the extent the owners of soybean meal choose not to engage in these transactions, they agree to forgo $794.60 of profit per 100 tons of soybean meal. In theory, the price of the futures contract should equal $19,164.60—the sum of $18,900, the spot price of 100 tons of soybean meal, and the financing cost of $264.60. But the market price is only $18,370, $794.60 less than the theoretical value.

How can we explain this discrepancy? The owners of soybean meal are willing to forgo the gain of $794.60 in exchange for the convenience of having soybean meal readily accessible, because during certain times of the year (prior to a harvest, for example) soybean meal is scarce. Because they need soybean meal to meet their customers' demands or for their own consumption, they are unwilling to part with it, even for a profit. We can think of this forgone profit as the premium the owners pay for accessibility. Arbitragers are unable to engage in transactions to correct the theoretical mispricing of the futures contracts, because they are unable to borrow the commodity from the owners. The forgone profit as a percentage of the spot price is called a *convenience yield.*

In order to determine the fair value of a commodity futures contract, we must reduce the cost of carry expressed as a percentage of the spot price by the convenience yield:

$$F = S \cdot e^{[(r - y) \cdot n/365]}$$

where

F = the fair value of a commodity futures contract,
S = the spot price of the underlying commodity,
e = the base of the natural logarithm (2.71828),
r = the annualized rate of total cost of carry including financing cost, insurance cost, storage cost and transportation cost,
y = the annualized convenience yield and
n = the number of days remaining until settlement date.

Investing in Commodity Futures Contracts

A commodity futures contract by itself is a highly leveraged investment. Purchasing a futures contract on a commodity is equivalent to acquiring the underlying commodity on margin. We can eliminate the inherent leverage of a futures position by collateralizing the position—that is, by investing an equivalent amount of funds in riskless securities. The lending implicit in a Treasury bill investment offsets the borrowing implicit in a futures contract investment.

The return on a collateralized futures portfolio consists of three components—the return on the underlying Treasury bill position, the return on the underlying commodity, and the *roll yield*, which is defined as the return from liquidating an existing futures position and establishing a new position in a contract with a more distant settlement date, controlling for the change in the spot price.

Should investors consider collateralized commodity futures positions as a potential investment?[6] The commodity component of the return on a collateralized futures portfolio offers superb diversification with respect to stocks and bonds. However, the long-run return from the underlying commodities may not be particularly appealing, because improvements in technology over time could increase the supply of commodities such as agricultural products and reduce the demand for commodities such as energy and industrial metals.

The roll yield component of the return on a commodity futures portfolio *may* offer an opportunity for investors to extract a premium by overweighting commodity futures contracts that are in backwardation (those that have positive roll yields) and underweighting commodity futures contracts that have negative roll yields.

As with most investment opportunities, commodity futures contracts present tradeoffs with respect to expected return and risk. Each investor should assess these within the context of his particular needs and attitude toward risk.

Notes

1. This article, of necessity, presents only a cursory description of commodity futures contracts. Those readers who wish a more detailed discussion of the topic are referred to F. Edwards and C. Ma, *Futures and Options* (New York: McGraw-Hill, Inc., 1992).

2. *Ibid.*, 6–9.

3. In this example and in those that follow, I ignore the effect of margin deposits.

4. *The Wall Street Journal*, December 17, 1992.

5. This profit estimate assumes that the only cost of carrying soybean meal is the interest cost.

6. For an excellent discussion of the investment suitability of commodities, see J. Scott, "Managing Asset Classes," *Financial Analysts Journal*, January/February 1994.

21
Currencies

As the trend toward globalization of financial markets persists, it is becoming imperative that financial analysts understand the available methods to control the risk from currency exposure or, alternatively, to profit from currency opportunities. Toward that end, this chapter is devoted to reviewing some of the key concepts and strategies of currency management and the more common instruments that are used to trade currencies.

Exchange Rates

To begin, it might be useful to review some of the terminology. One of the most basic notions is the exchange rate. The spot exchange rate is the rate at which one currency can be exchanged for another currency, typically for settlement in two days.

The international convention, except in the cases of the British pound and the Australian dollar, is to quote exchange rates with the U.S. dollar as the base currency. For domestic transactions within the U.S., however, exchange rates are often quoted as U.S. dollar-equivalent rates, with the dollar as the variable currency.

For example, as of 3 p.m. eastern standard time on December 4, 1991, the spot rate to exchange U.S. dollars for deutschmarks was 0.6236. In other words, as of that moment, traders were willing to exchange 0.6236 dollars for one mark to be settled in two business days. The reciprocal of this, the mark-equivalent exchange rate, equaled 1.6036. The spot rate to exchange British pounds as of the same date and time equaled 1.7810.

From these values, we can infer the cross rate between the mark and the pound. Since the spot rate to exchange dollars for marks was 0.6236, while the spot rate to exchange dollars for pounds was 1.7810, the spot rate to exchange pounds for marks equaled 0.3501. This is found by dividing 0.6236 by 1.7810.

This rate is expressed in pound-equivalent terms. We can infer the mark-equivalent cross rate by dividing the dollar-equivalent pound exchange rate by the dollar-equivalent mark exchange rate or, of course, by computing the reciprocal of the pound-equivalent cross rate.

The forward exchange rate is the rate agreed to today at which a currency can be exchanged for another currency at a more distant future date. Taking our earlier example of the dollar and mark on December 4, 1991, the dollar-equivalent 30-day forward exchange rate was 0.6213. The reciprocal, with the dollar as the base currency, was 1.6095. The one-month forward rate to exchange dollars for British pounds at this time was 1.7729. The cross rate—the one-month forward rate to change pounds for marks—thus equaled 0.3504.

Interest Rate Parity

The dollar-equivalent one-month forward rate to exchange dollars for marks was slightly lower than the spot rate (0.6213 versus 0.6236). Conversely, the mark-equivalent one-month forward rate to exchange marks for pounds was slightly higher than the spot rate (0.3504 versus 0.3501). Therefore, the forward price of the mark is at a discount to the dollar and at a premium to the pound.

These relationships are explained by the most important theory of foreign exchange—the theory of interest rate parity. This theory has two variations—covered interest rate parity, which is really an arbitrage condition, and uncovered interest rate parity, which is sometimes used to forecast future spot rates.

To understand the theory of covered interest rate parity, suppose that the one-year riskless rate of interest is 5 percent in the U.S. and 10 percent in the U.K., and that the dollar-equivalent spot exchange rate is 1.80. The forward exchange rate must equal the rate that would preclude an arbitrageur from borrowing in the U.S. at 5 percent and lending in the U.K. at 10 percent without incurring risk. An arbitrageur would hedge away risk by selling the pound forward one year in an amount equal to the amount that must be repaid in one year.

Suppose, for example, the arbitrageur borrows 1 million dollars in the U.S. at 5 percent and converts this sum to 555,556 pounds in the U.K. at 10 percent. Simultaneously, she sells 600,000 pounds one year forward at a rate of 1.75, which is equivalent to the 1,050,000 dollars required to repay the 1 million dollar loan at 5 percent interest. These transactions would result in a profit of 18,889 dollars should the pound decline to 1.70 dollars one year from now and 21,111 dollars should it increase to 1.90 dollars one year from now, as Table 21.1 shows.

Regardless of whether the pound rises or falls, the arbitrageur profits from these transactions, given a forward exchange rate of 1.75. If the forward rate were 1.69, the arbitrageur could still profit—by reversing the above transactions.

From these examples, it appears that there is some forward rate between 1.69 and 1.75 at which an arbitrageur would neither profit nor lose by borrowing in one country, lending in another and hedging away the currency risk. This rate is found by multiplying the current spot rate by the quantity one plus the U.S. interest rate divided by one plus the U.K. interest rate. In our example, this rate equals 1.7182:

$$1.80 \cdot (1.05/1.10) = 1.7182$$

Essentially, the cost of hedging away the currency risk of a country with a high interest rate exactly offsets the advantage of lending at the higher interest rate. Table 21.2 shows that a forward rate equal to 1.7182 will preclude arbitrage profits or losses regardless of subsequent changes in the spot rate.

One might argue that, given a significant interest rate differential, it may make sense to borrow in the low-interest-rate country and lend in the high-interest-rate country, without hedging away the currency exposure. If future spot rates fluctuate randomly around the current spot rate, then such a strategy might make sense over the long run or across several pairs of high and low-interest-rate countries. We would then be gaining a certain interest rate advantage

---

Table 21.1 Arbitrage Payoffs at Pound-Dollar Spot Rate of 1.80 and Forward Rate of 1.75

	Pound Declines to 1.70	Pound Increases to 1.90
Interest Cost	$50,000	$ 50,000
Proceeds from Loan	94,444	105,556
Profit/Loss on Principal	−55,556	55,556
Profit/Loss on Hedge	30,000	−90,000
Net Profit/Loss	18,889	21,111

Table 21.2 Arbitrage Payoffs at Pound-Dollar Spot Rate of 1.80 and Forward Rate of 1.7182

	Pound Declines to 1.70	Pound Decline to 1.90
Interest Cost	$50,000	$ 50,000
Proceeds from Loan	94,444	105,556
Profit/Loss on Principal	−55,556	55,556
Profit/Loss on Hedge	11,111	−111,111
Net Profit/Loss	0	0

with an expected but uncertain currency loss of zero (assuming the current spot rate represents the central tendency of future spot rates).

This leads us to the second variation of interest rate parity—uncovered interest rate parity. If on balance, speculators do not pursue such unhedged strategies, we might infer that they expect the currencies of the high-interest-rate countries to fall relative to the currencies of the low-interest-rate countries. Moreover, the level to which they must fall so that there is no expected profit or loss is precisely the current forward rate. The forward rate is said to be an "unbiased estimate" of the future spot rate.

This is the theory of uncovered interest rate parity. It does not suggest that the forward rate is a particularly accurate forecast of the future spot rate; it merely holds that it does not systematically over- or underforecast subsequent changes in the spot rate.

Trading Currencies

Currencies are traded on exchanges and by private negotiation. The preponderance of volume in currencies is transacted in the interbank market through the use of forward contracts. A forward contract is a privately negotiated contract between two parties obligating the seller to pay the value of the contract to the buyer at a specified date. If one party wishes to nullify a contract prior to expiration, he or she must enter into another forward contract to offset the exposure of the first contract.

It is conventional for dealers to quote forward contracts in terms of a forward rate's discount or premium to the spot rate. This is because the spot rate may change significantly during the few minutes it takes a trader to call several dealers to obtain the best quote, whereas the discount or premium component of the forward rate is more stable.

Futures contracts serve as an alternative to forward contracts for some of the major currencies, including the pound, the mark, the French franc, the Swiss franc, the yen and the Canadian and Australian dollars, which are traded on the Chicago Mercantile Exchange. These contracts also obligate the seller to pay the value of the contract to the buyer at a specified date, but they differ from forward contracts in that they have uniform terms regarding price, quantity and expiration. There is thus an active secondary market in which traders can buy and sell futures contracts. This secondary market makes it easier to nullify or reverse an earlier trade. Futures contracts are disadvantaged relative to forward contracts, however, in that it is more difficult to customize a position using futures contracts. Furthermore, futures contracts require initial margin as well as variation margin to cover daily price fluctuations, whereas forward contracts do not require margin deposits from creditworthy traders.

Perhaps the most relevant distinction between forward and futures contracts is the differential cost of executing a trade with these instruments. It is typically cheaper to execute small trades of major currencies in the futures market, while it is cheaper to execute large trades in the forward market. The reason for this differential is that the forward market handles much more volume than the futures market, so it is less sensitive to market impact from large trades. But the forward market is also a volume discount market, and this penalizes small trades. The definition of a small versus a large trade is not cast in stone. As a rule of thumb, though, multimillion dollar trades can usually be executed at a lower price in the forward market, while trades of less than a million dollars can often be executed less expensively in the futures market.

When we use forward or futures contracts to offset a currency exposure, we eliminate currency risk. At the same time, however, we sacrifice any potential profit from a favorable currency price change. To overcome this regret factor, we can hedge our currency risk and still preserve the opportunity to benefit from a favorable price shift by using currency options.

Exchange-traded options are available for a small number of currencies. American options, which carry the right to exercise the option at any time up to expiration, are traded on the Philadelphia Stock Exchange for the pound, the mark, the French franc, the Swiss franc, the yen and the Australian dollar. European options, which can only be exercised at expiration, are traded on the Philadelphia Stock Exchange for the pound, the mark and the Swiss franc. Exchange-traded options are also available on currency futures contracts. These options, which are American in type, are traded on the Chicago Mercantile Exchange for futures contracts on the pound, the mark, the Swiss franc, the yen and the Canadian and Australian dollars. Options on currencies derive their value from the spot exchange rate, whereas options on currency future contracts derive their value from the price of the underlying futures contracts. In addition to exchange-traded currency options, there is a vast over-the-counter market that accommodates the demand for options on non-exchange-traded currencies and customized options.

The valuation of a currency option is analogous to the valuation of a dividend-paying asset. The foreign interest rate is treated as a dividend yield. An American currency option may trade at a higher price than a European currency option with equivalent terms, because it may be advantageous to exercise the option early.[1]

We can also manage currency exposure through the use of currency swaps. This term is applied to several types of transactions. Typically, the term swap refers to an arrangement in which a party agrees to purchase or sell a currency on one date and reverse the transaction at a specified future date. The swap rate, which is the difference between the exchange rate used in the two trades, is agreed upon in advance.

Another variation of a currency swap is an exchange of liabilities between parties in different countries. For example, a U.S. company might need to borrow funds in Germany but may not wish to incur the risk that the dollar could decline during the term of the loan. The U.S. company can seek a German counterpart that needs funds in the U.S. and exchange these liabilities at the prevailing exchange rate. Under a swap arrangement, if one of the parties defaults, the other is automatically released from its obligation. Essentially, a currency swap is tantamount to a series of forward contracts that hedge the interest payments as well as the principal repayment. This hedging is accomplished with a single transaction, however.[2]

To Hedge or Not to Hedge

Empirical evidence for the most part indicates that diversification into foreign assets improves the risk-return tradeoff of a securities portfolio. This evidence is sometimes misconstrued, though, to imply that exposure to currencies necessarily lowers portfolio risk. This fallacy rests on the assumption that currencies have low correlations with other portfolio assets and therefore provide diversification benefits. The problem with this reasoning is that it ignores the fact that currency exposure introduces uncertainty as well as diversification.

To see the total impact of currency exposure on portfolio risk, suppose that we have a portfolio equally divided between a single domestic asset and a single foreign asset and that both assets have standard deviations of 20 percent and are uncorrelated with each other. (The foreign asset's returns are denominated in the domestic currency.) Let us further suppose that the standard deviation of a forward contract on the currency is 15 percent and that it is uncorrelated with the domestic asset.

Now let us explore three situations. In the first, the currency is uncorrelated with the foreign asset.[3] In the second, it is 50 percent correlated with the foreign asset. In the third, it is 75 percent correlated with the foreign asset. Table 21.3 shows the results of an unhedged, fully hedged, and optimally hedged portfolio.

In the situation in which the currency is uncorrelated with the foreign asset, the optimal strategy is to accept all the currency exposure from the foreign asset.[4] The intuition here is straightforward. The foreign asset's return is denominated in the domestic currency;

Table 21.3 Portfolio Risk (Standard Deviation) as a Function of Currency Exposure

	Correlation with Foreign Asset				
	0%		50%		75%
Unhedged	14.14%		14.14%		14.14%
Fully Hedged	16.60		13.46		10.31
Optimally Hedged*	14.14	(0%)	13.23	(67%)	10.31	(100%)

* Optimal percentage to hedge is shown in parentheses.

hence, by definition, part of the foreign asset's return is the currency's return. Therefore, in order for the currency to be uncorrelated with the foreign asset's domestic return, it must be negatively correlated with the foreign asset's local return. In this case, the currency exposure hedges the foreign asset's local return and benefits the overall portfolio.

In the case in which the currency is 50 percent correlated with the foreign asset's return (denominated in the domestic currency), currency exposure does not hedge the foreign asset's local return sufficiently to offset the volatility it introduces to the overall portfolio. It is thus worthwhile to hedge some of the currency exposure.

In the situation in which the currency is 75 percent correlated with the foreign asset's return, the optimal strategy is to hedge away all the embedded currency exposure of the foreign asset.

These results, of course, are specific to the example described above. It is generally the case, however, that a portfolio in which the embedded currency exposure is hedged away will be less risky than an unhedged portfolio. Furthermore, there is usually some degree of hedging less than full hedging that optimally balances a currency's diversification properties with the uncertainty it introduces to the portfolio such that we can reduce portfolio risk even further. Finally, the decision of whether or not to hedge a portfolio's currency risk should reflect a realistic assessment of the costs of hedging this risk.

Currency Anomalies

Researchers in both the academic and practitioner communities have discovered special tendencies of currencies. Empirical evidence suggests that the forward rate does not behave in accordance with the theory of uncovered interest rate parity. (The evidence does not violate covered interest rate parity, however.) Contrary to theory, the implicit forecast of the forward rate systematically exaggerates subsequent changes in the spot rate. The obvious implication of this evidence is that traders willing to incur risk can profit, on average, by purchasing forward contracts on currencies of high-interest-rate countries (those that sell at a forward discount) and by selling forward contracts on currencies of low-interest-rate countries (those that sell at a forward premium).[5]

A second anomalous tendency of currencies is that their returns tend to be positively serially correlated. This tendency is independent of the forward rate bias in that the effect persists whether currency returns are derived from spot rates or from forward rates. Positive serial correlation, which we can state more prosaically as trends, suggests that investors can profit from trading rules that call for acquiring currencies as they appreciate and selling currencies as they depreciate.[6] We would be well advised to temper our enthusiasm about these anomalies, however, because the evidence is based on a relatively short history compared with that of other financial assets. It was only in the mid '70s that currency exchange rates were allowed to float.

Notes

1. For an excellent review of currency options, see R. Stapleton and C. Thanassoulas, "Options on Foreign Currencies," in Figlewski, Silber and Subrahmanyam, eds., *Financial Options: From Theory to Practice* (Homewood, IL: Business One Irwin, 1990).

2. For a more detailed review of currency swaps and other currency related instruments, see B. Solnik, *International Investments*, second edition (New York: Addison-Wesley Publishing Company, 1991), pp. 176–183.

3. Within this context, the term currency is used to refer to a forward contract on the currency.

4. The optimal hedge ratio is the percentage of the embedded currency exposure that is sold short, holding constant the other portfolio assets, so that total portfolio risk is minimized. For a discussion of the determination of the optimal hedge ratio, see M. Kritzman, "A Simple Solution for Optimal Currency Hedging," *Financial Analysts Journal*, November/December 1989.

5. For a discussion of forward rate bias and a trading strategy to exploit it, see P. Green, "Is Currency Trading Profitable? Exploiting Deviations from Uncovered Interest Parity," *Financial Analysts Journal*, forthcoming.

6. This phenomenon is described in C. Engel and J. Hamilton, "Long Swings in the Dollar: Are They in the Data and Do

Markets Know It?" *American Economic Review*, September 1990, pp. 689–712. Further evidence of serial dependence and its implications is discussed in M. Kritzman, "Serial Dependence in Currency Returns: Investment Implications," *Journal of Portfolio Management*, Fall 1989.

Index